Before All Hell Breaks Loose

KEN HUTCHERSON

BEFORE ALL HELL BREAKS LOOSE

Multnomah® Publishers *Sisters, Oregon*

BEFORE ALL HELL BREAKS LOOSE
published by Multnomah Publishers, Inc.

© 2001 by Ken Hutcherson

International Standard Book Number: 1-57673-793-4

Cover photo of the church by Charles Benes\Index Stock Imagery
Background cover image by Tony Stone Images

Unless otherwise noted, Scripture quotations are from:
The Holy Bible, New King James Version © 1984 by Thomas Nelson, Inc.

Also quoted:
New American Standard Bible (NASB) © 1960, 1977, 1995
by the Lockman Foundation. Used by permission.

The Holy Bible, New International Version (NIV) © 1973, 1984 by International Bible
Society, used by permission of Zondervan Publishing House.

Holy Bible, New Living Translation (NLT) © 1996. Used by permission of Tyndale
House Publishers, Inc. All rights reserved.

Multnomah is a trademark of Multnomah Publishers, Inc.,
and is registered in the U.S. Patent and Trademark Office.
The colophon is a trademark of Multnomah Publishers, Inc.

Printed in the United States of America

01 02 03 04 05—10 9 8 7 6 5 4 3 2 1 0

Dedication

To all the members of Antioch Bible Church,
who have endured years of my preaching.
To my wife, Pat, who has had to share her husband
with thousands every week for the past fifteen years.
To my children, Faith, Avery, Sherman, and Curtis,
who have put up with their father's bad jokes and tricks
and have loved me anyway.
To all of you I want to say thank you, and that I love you deeply.
To you I dedicate this work.

CONTENTS

YOU'VE GOT MAIL!

What does the church think about Jesus?

That's the question upon which we spend most of our time, isn't it? Preachers strain so that we'll fix our eyes on Jesus; we read books to align our lives with Scripture; we meditate in prayer, seeking the mind of Christ. Much of what we do in our Christian walk is designed to make certain we're thinking right things about our Lord.

What do we think about Jesus?

That's a good question.

But it's not the only question.

There's another question in the early chapters of the book of Revelation that has a way of jumping up off the page and grabbing us by the throat. And it is this:

What does Jesus think about the church?

What does He think about the passion, purity, and priorities of individual believers? Is He pleased with what He sees today? Is He grieved? Is He angry? What would He say to us—right now, today—if He chose to speak about the true heart condition of believers in the contemporary church?

Guess what?

That's just what He has done.

In chapters 2 and 3 of Revelation, the living, resurrected Lord of the church appears on earth in majesty and glory and dictates seven letters to seven churches. Contained within those little letters are awesome promises, smokin' warnings, and straight talk to believers—all as up-to-date as *CNN Headline News*.

We can find ourselves in all seven letters.

Like the Christians in Ephesus, we too sometimes major in the minors and forget our first love.

Some of us have tasted persecution for following God's will, like Smyrna.

We understand Pergamum's hypocrisy all too well—standing firm against Satan one minute, tolerating gross sin the next.

We have to admit in our hearts that Thyatira didn't corner the market on sexual impurity.

Like Sardis, we sometimes find ourselves coasting along on our good reputations, while inside our spiritual lives are as cold as the ashes from last week's fire.

And do we know what Jesus was talking about when He warned Laodicea about lukewarm hearts? I think we understand Him just fine on that score.

Jesus appears in the Gospels as the Lamb of God who takes away the sin of the world. But in Revelation He comes as King of kings and Lord of lords. He comes as righteous judge; in Revelation 2 and 3, He makes sober pronouncements about His sometimes wayward subjects.

But just as Jesus had hard words for His churches, He also had powerful words of hope. Do this, He said to them (and to us), and you will live. "Come back to Me, your first love. Wash your garments; strengthen the things that remain; and open the door to Me. Overcome and I will give you the crown of eternal life."

The churches in Asia Minor were small—possibly no larger than house churches. Yet the risen Christ walked among them; the Son of God held them in the palm of His hand. Our Lord's words to these seven little churches occupy two whole chapters of Scripture. These churches may have been small in the eyes of men, but they were not small in the eyes of God.

And neither are we.

Each of those churches lives in our midst. And the same Jesus Christ—the Eternal One, the Alpha and the Omega—has a message of love and warning to today's believers.

In this book we're going to look at those seven churches and find ourselves in each. We'll copy what they're doing right and stay clear of what Jesus rebuked them for. We'll feel the double-edged sword cut us to the quick and see that the Alpha and the Omega holds the keys to our recovery.

If we've lost our love, it's time to repent! If we're facing pressure and persecution, it's time to focus on the One who overcomes. If we find ourselves surrounded by a decadent culture, it's time to hate the things He hates! If we find ourselves trapped by immoral thoughts and habits, it's time to come clean and take a fresh grip on the truth. If we've allowed the life of Christ to ebb away from our hearts, it's time to wake up and find Him again. If we're tired of just hanging in there, it's time to tap into His mighty power. If we think we're prosperous, safe, and can move into heaven on cruise control, we'd better check with the Lord of the church and see if He is of the same opinion.

You've got mail, Jack.

Seven letters have been waiting in your box.

I can't think of a better time to open them than right now.

CHAPTER ONE

SPECIAL DELIVERY

Suppose you're at home with your family having one of those rare quiet evenings. You've put dinner away, and now you're all kicked back in the living room talking quietly about the day. Soft music plays in the background, and a fire crackles in the fireplace.

Suddenly a stranger throws open the front door and says, "I want to talk to y'all!"

Now, I don't know what you would do if someone did that in your house, but I know what I would do. I'd say to my rottweilers, "Sic 'em, sic 'em, sic 'em!" (It would all be done in Christian love, don't you know! Ripped to ribbons in the name of God.)

Let's say this stranger comes up to you and starts telling you what you need to do about your family. You've never seen this guy before. You don't know who he is; you don't know if he's dangerous; you don't know what kind of family he comes from. As far as you know he has no authority to tell you how to run your family.

How would you react? Would you be excited about this guy coming in uninvited, wanting to tell you what you need to do for your family? Would you say, "Oh, he must be sent from God"? Or would you say, "Get outta my house!"?

Maybe you're so loving and sensitive that you would open your arms to this intruder that's shoving his way into your house and telling you what to do. All right, think about this: What if you were at the hospital having open-heart surgery? As the surgeon carefully operates on you, some street person who happens to be passing by the hospital hears that you are being operated on bursts into the room, rushes up to the doctor, and says, "Hey, hey, hey! You don't know what you're doin'. Let *me* finish this operation!"

Now, would you be excited about that? I don't care if they had put you under—that would wake you up! A hobo off the street has no authority in an operating room; the surgeon has the authority. A stranger has no authority in your home; your family has the authority. So when someone in the family speaks, it carries some clout. When the surgeon performing the operation speaks, his word counts because he has authority to be there and authority to know what needs to be done.

That's what's happening in Revelation. Jesus Christ is bustin' through into our world to tell His household what it needs to do.

And He has a perfect right to do that very thing.

Why? Because He is the Bridegroom, the head of the bride. He needs no invitation because He *belongs* there. All authority has been given to Him by the Father. He who is the head of all believers is saying something to the church in Revelation 2 and 3, and the church had better listen.

NOT WITH A FEATHER

The first time Jesus came to earth, He came in humility: born in a stable, raised in a humble home, and working with Joseph in the carpenter's shop. He came to serve and to give Himself as a ransom.

Not so the second time.

When He comes back this time, He'll come to *be* served. He won't be coming back to die, but to sweep His enemies right off the planet. He will be glorified beyond anything on this earth. That's how we see Him in Revelation.

The Jesus of Revelation is the risen Messiah, the Lion of Judah, the King of kings and Lord of lords. He is the Alpha and Omega, the beginning and end, the holder of the keys of death and Hades. His voice is like the sound of mighty waters, His eyes are like flame, and His face shines like the sun. Out of His mouth comes the two-edged sword of the Word of God. He is the holy invader, the first and the last, and the righteous Judge before whose gaze you will fall to the ground as if dead.

And listen, this isn't some picture of Jesus in the sweet by-and-by. This is Jesus right now! And even though He is coming again to take charge on this planet, He comes right now to take charge in your life! Get ready—He comes to you and me every day of our lives and says, "I am the glorified Jesus Christ, the Son of God who died on the cross for you. I am the beginning and the end. I last forever. I was before *before* and I'm going to be after *after*. Wake up! I'm coming back. And it's not going to be with a feather this time. You better be on My side before I get there, because I'm not coming like I've ever come before. And by the way, I'm never going to leave again."

He's coming with all authority! Just take a look at Jesus' feet as He appears to John on Patmos: "His feet were like fine brass, as if refined in a furnace" (Revelation 1:15). In New Testament times when a subject came before a king, he couldn't be on the same level with him. The best that could be hoped for was to be level with the king's feet. Feet speak of authority: judging authority, conquering authority.

Now, I don't know about you, but if the Messiah is coming, I don't want to be under His feet as His enemy; I want to be behind Him as part of His army. Are you at the Lord's feet for the right purpose today? Would He say that you are on His side? You can fall at His feet to worship, or you can be crushed by His feet in judgment. Either way, you have to deal with those feet. You'd better get it right, because that's how the Messiah's coming.

SETTING THE STAGE

When John received the Revelation, the church was at one of its lowest points in history. John was the last apostle still living. The rest were dead—and none of them had died of old age! Every one of them had been martyred. Peter had said he wasn't worthy to be crucified like Christ, so they crucified him upside down. Many of the apostles had been beheaded, and others were ripped apart or skinned alive. This was not a very good time to be in the church. Folks weren't holding Christmas bazaars in church parking lots, I can tell you that much. It was a very, very dangerous time to admit you belonged to Jesus Christ.

But John was still alive. Why? I can only think of one reason: He hadn't written the book of Revelation yet. His example clearly indicates that as long as the Lord has work for you to accomplish on earth, no one can stop you!

Not that they didn't try to kill him. The Romans hated Christians with a passion. Emperor Nero had passed a law that made Christianity an illegal religion. Nero was so bad that he would take possession of Christians that had been thrown into jail, and during his parties he would dip them in wax and set them afire so they would provide light for his guests to see by.

I'm going to tell you a secret right now: You can be light for God, or you can let the world make you a light. One way is glorious; the other way hurts!

One story told about John during this time of persecution is that the Romans plunged him into boiling oil, and he came out unhurt. God saved his life. Later, they exiled him to the isle of Patmos because of the One he claimed as Lord.

So take a look: The church was seeing Christians persecuted, all the apostles who walked with Christ martyred, and the very last one packed off into exile. Do you think that the church was having a little bit of a problem singing "Stand up, Stand up for Jesus"?

The church was compromising because it was afraid to stand up. The church was screaming, "Where are You, Lord? We're down here dying for You. We've stood up for You. But now everything is miserable."

Have you ever felt that way? Husband, have you ever felt like you stood up for Christ and the only thing you got was pie on your face? Wife, have you felt that you wanted to be a godly woman and the only thing you got was footprints all over your body? Maybe you stood for

Christ as an employee and were fired; perhaps you stood for Christ as an employer and are in trouble for it. Where is God?

"I'm standing up for You, Lord, and You're up there in heaven somewhere thinking everything's okay. You'd better get down here and see what's happening to Your kids!" Have you ever felt like that?

What are Jesus' first words when He comes to John? He says, "I haven't forgotten you. I'm coming back. And I want you to hold on."

But the believers were feeling forgotten, all the same. You have to remember that the seven churches of Revelation were no megachurches. They didn't have TV ministries, multimember staffs, or fancy suburban campuses with sculptures and fountains all around. They weren't breaking attendance records. The town mayor wasn't on the church roll. These were house churches—probably no more than ten or twelve folks each. Most people didn't even know they were there. If the world ever did notice them, it didn't line up to sing their praises. It was more along the lines of, "Hey, Nero's got another party comin' up!"

But look who *did* know they were there!

They didn't rate on earth, but I'm telling you that they featured big in heaven. Someone powerful had His eye on them, and for these tiny little groups of weak believers, forgotten and unnoticed by the world, He was about to move heaven and earth.

Seals would be opened. The heavens would proceed to shake. The sun would darken, and the stars would fall. Mountains and islands were about to be moved from their places. Trumpets would blow, turning the very rain to hail, fire, and blood. God was about to open the pit and fill the earth with woe. Battles would be fought in heaven and on earth, vials of wrath emptied, and scenes enacted over which heaven would shout hallelujah.

But before it all and above it all, the mind of the great Judge, the risen Jesus Christ Almighty, was set on His little company of believers; to them He gave His first attention. Hallelujah, what a Savior!

You husbands and wives, you employees and employers, you persecuted and beaten down who feel like God has forgotten you: Lift up your heads! The Alpha and the Omega, the One who was before *before* and will be after *after,* has His mind set on you. And for you He's going to bring it all crashing down around the heads of evildoers. For you, dear children, for you.

SPIRITS, STARS, AND LAMPSTANDS

Before we get rolling down the Revelation highway, I want to solve two mysteries about John's vision. One, what in the world does Revelation 1:4 mean when it talks about the seven Spirits who are before His throne? And two, what does verse 20 mean when it talks about the seven stars and the seven lampstands? First, the seven Spirits:

> John, to the seven churches which are in Asia:
>
> Grace to you and peace from Him who is and who was and who is to come, and from the seven Spirits who are before His throne, and from Jesus Christ, the faithful witness, the firstborn from the dead, and the ruler over the kings of the earth. To Him who loved us and washed us from our sins in His own blood. (Revelation 1:4–5)

At first I thought verse 4 was talking about Jesus—"Him who is and who was and who is to come"—but now I believe this is God the Father. Why? Because we've got the whole Trinity here. Look: We've got God the Father, who is and was and is to come. We've got Jesus Christ, the faithful witness. And we've got the Holy Spirit—depicted, I believe, by the seven Spirits that are before the throne.

Go back with me to Isaiah 11. As you read this passage, keep in mind that the number seven is the perfect number for God.

> There shall come forth a Rod from the stem of Jesse,
> And a Branch shall grow out of his roots.
> The Spirit of the LORD shall rest upon Him,
> The Spirit of wisdom and understanding,
> The Spirit of counsel and might,
> The Spirit of knowledge and of the fear of the LORD.
> (vv. 1–2)

"And the Spirit of the LORD shall rest upon Him." That's one—the Spirit of the Lord. Then there's the Spirit of wisdom; that's two. The Spirit of understanding is number three. The Spirit of counsel, the Spirit of might, the Spirit of knowledge, and the Spirit of the fear of the Lord are four, five, six, and…seven. Well, what do you know? Seven spirits of God. But we know that's just a fancy way of talking about the one Holy Spirit, right?

Now when we look back at Revelation 1:4–5 we begin to see what's going on. Seven Spirits of God? Or one Holy Spirit present in each of the seven churches of Asia Minor? Call it the sevenfold Spirit of God.

If there are one billion Christians and they all have the Holy Spirit, there aren't one billion Holy Spirits. There's just one, broken into one billion believers. He's the billionfold Holy Spirit. Every church has the Holy Spirit, too. That's what I believe we're seeing with this seven Spirits thing.

Second, what's with the seven stars and the seven lampstands? John says,

> "The mystery of the seven stars which you saw in My right hand, and the seven golden lampstands: The seven stars are the angels of the seven churches, and the seven lampstands which you saw are the seven churches." (Revelation 1:20)

The seven stars are the angels of the seven churches. What are messengers? *Those who bring messages.* And what are angels but messengers? I believe these seven messengers are the seven *leaders* of the churches in Asia Minor.

Jesus speaks to the leaders of the seven churches because as the leader is, so is the church. Everything Jesus says in chapters 2 and 3 is directed to the churches, but His words have to first rest on the seven leaders of those churches. If they had been doing what they were supposed to do, they wouldn't have needed Jesus to bust in and tell 'em what's what like He did.

So the seven Spirits are really the Holy Spirit, making Revelation a vision from the whole Trinity, and the seven stars are the leaders of the churches, represented by the seven lampstands. Clear as chocolate milk?

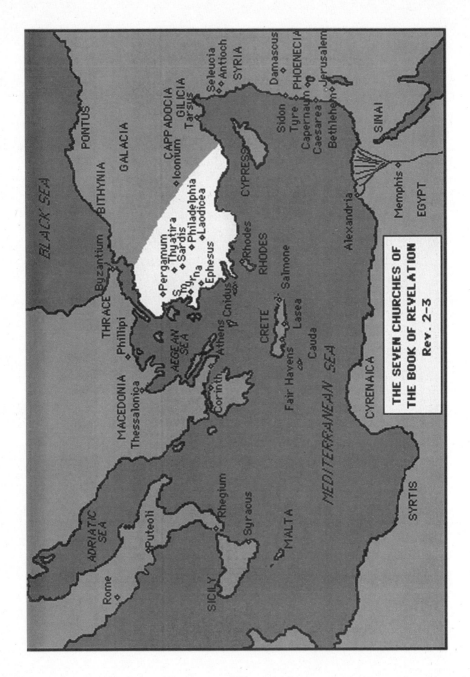

SCOUTING OUT THE CHURCHES

Take a look at the map below. This is Asia Minor, also known as modern-day Turkey. Do you see how the churches are laid out in relation to one another? It's amazing how God through His Revelation established the order of the churches. The order of the letters in Revelation 2 and 3 most likely mirrors the route a messenger would take if he were traveling through the countryside.

Do you see little Patmos there? That's where John was when he received the Revelation. He'd been an elder in Ephesus for many years, but had recently been exiled to Patmos. Needless to say, Ephesus was heavy on his mind.

Ephesus was the place where a messenger would strike land to start out across country. At that time it was the most important city in Asia Minor, though it was not the capital. After Ephesus, a traveler would move up to Smyrna. Then he would take the letter to Pergamum, then over to Thyatira, then Sardis, to the church of Philadelphia, then on to Laodicea.

Now, I want you to see how smokin' God is. Not only is there a geographical reason as to why the letters to the churches fall in the order they do; there's also a theological reason. Check this out.

Ephesus and Laodicea are the first and the seventh churches, right across from each other geographically. They also have a very similar problem: They are the worst of the churches. Of the seven they are the two coldest. Next you can see that Smyrna and Philadelphia are across from each other. They are the second and the sixth churches—and they're also the best ones, the most on fire for God. Is He awesome or what?

Which are left? Pergamum, Thyatira, and Sardis, right in the middle. They are the lukewarm churches. Geographically and theologically, they're smack-dab in the middle of the others, neither hot nor cold.

I think God orchestrated this so that you and I would understand that we should be either hot or cold, because He hates lukewarm! You need to make that decision personally. Are you going to be hot or cold for God?

Let me give you a couple of examples to relate to: Lukewarm espresso makes you want to gag; lukewarm hot tubs are worse than useless. So why would anyone think that being a lukewarm Christian would please God?

THAT WAS THEN, THIS IS NOW

The most awesome thing about the letters to the seven churches is that they were really written to us, too. This is the Bridegroom speaking words of instruction, correction, and encouragement to His bride. So long as we're in the church age—everything between the Pentecost and the Rapture—these words apply to us.

These are letters for you and me, waiting in our private mailboxes—priority e-mails stacked up in our server.

The church age is the only period in biblical prophecy that does not have a set time limit. God knows the time span; He just hasn't given it to us. After the church age is over—start the countdown!—the earth has only 1,007 years left. We're heading for the seven-year wrath of God, called the Tribulation, and the thousand-year reign of God, the millennial period, when saints will reign with Christ. After God raptures this church out of here, the earth as we know it will have 1,007 years left to spin on its axis.

Now, maybe you're saying, "Shoot, I've got plenty of time." Wait a minute: I said the earth has 1,007 years; I didn't say *you* did! Hopefully you make it to the bottom of this page!

Revelation 2 and 3 are in the middle, just as the church age is the middle dispensation. This is perhaps better understood when we see that Revelation 1 is based upon that which Jesus has seen—it portrays Him as ruler of all the world—and that chapters 4 through 22 are all about that which will happen when the last days come. They look at Jesus Christ as the coming King, the Judge who will rule with an iron hand. But Revelation 2 and 3 are based upon that which is happening right now. They depict Jesus Christ as the Bridegroom, the head of the church.

"Wait, Hutch," you may be saying. "These letters were written to seven *historical* churches. How can you say they're for us today?" *That's* an easy one. Most of Scripture was written to a historical audience, but still applies to us. Take Luke's Gospel: It was written to one man, the most excellent Theophilus, so he could know the truth of what he'd been taught. But that doesn't stop believers from opening their Bibles to Luke and reading about the Prodigal Son, does it? That's the beauty of Scripture: It's relevant for all ages and peoples.

So here in Revelation 2 and 3 the Bridegroom, He who is the head of all believers, is speaking to the church—and that means all of the church, so long as believers still walk the earth. And the church would do well to pay attention.

These letters to the churches are precious. Like the parables, they're made up entirely of Christ's own words. And they're among the very last words that were given directly from Him. In fact, they may be the only unabridged record of His addresses.

As you read, ask yourself, "Does my life line up with any of these seven churches? Do I have some of the same problems in my life that were found in these churches? Does what the head of the church commands them to do fit with what I need to do to get right with Him?"

Jesus Christ is bustin' into your life today. He's breaking in because He wants to tell you how to live, to encourage you in your struggles, and to let you know He hasn't forgotten you.

You may not feel that you stack up very well against many of the people you know. You may feel like small potatoes. But it isn't true. If the Son of God has His eye on you, if the Almighty has taken the time to send you some highly personal mail, it doesn't matter what the rest of the world thinks.

If you're on the mind of God, if you're in the thoughts of heaven, you have value and significance beyond your wildest dreams. What are you going to do with it?

Now let him who has ears to hear, hear what the Spirit says to the churches!

CHAPTER TWO

Ephesus:
WASTED POTENTIAL

Your first love.

Three simple words. What kind of picture do those words paint in your mind? What is that thing or person that makes it worthwhile for you to roll out of bed in the morning? How do you describe that activity or relationship that lights your fire, floats your boat, makes the stars come out at night?

What holds that *numero uno* place in your heart? What is it that gives your life meaning? A person? A fishin' boat? A big, black, mean Dodge pickup? Hittin' the malls with time to burn and a shiny new credit card in your hot little hand?

Your first love. Can you remember?

Maybe you had it and married it.

Maybe you had it and lost it.

Maybe you had it only in your dreams.

And if you're a certain age, maybe you've just *had* it!

But do you remember that wonderful person of the opposite sex that just made you *oooh?* The words aren't even there, but you know the person that made you just kind of *oooh!* You loved him or her, loved just being around him or her, do you remember? (Can your old gray cells reach back that far?)

There was the guy that made you have goo-goo eyes, who made you feel kind of schoolgirlish all over again. You loved him so much that you would even go to one of those monster truck shows and enjoy it! You didn't care; you didn't even notice all the mud and noise and clouds of exhaust—because you were with him.

"Hey, the trucks are out there," he'd say, pointing.

"I know," you'd answer, "but what I like is right here."

You ignored the inconveniences because with your first love you enjoyed anything, just so long as you were together.

Or there was that girl that you loved so much you would even go with her to watch a movie like *Love Story.* (I know you went to some of those chick flicks, so don't try to tell me you didn't.) She was right there next to you, and she smelled *good.* Whew! You were so in love that you didn't care where you were or what the movie was; you were just glad to be with her. You could reach over and touch her when you wanted to. (Uh-oh. Hold on. That touchin' stuff can get a lot of Christian guys in trouble, so watch out what you touch—you know what I'm talking about!)

ONE FATEFUL DAY

Then one day something changed. "Monster trucks?" she said disdainfully. "I don't want to go watch monster trucks. You never think about what I want to do!"

And you're left asking yourself, "Is this the same woman I married?"

Or he says, *"Love Story?* Forget it! All that lovey-dovey, explore-your-feelings, Jane Austen stuff? No, no, no, no. Give me an action flick. I want to see someone's head get busted. I want to see some buildings get blown up!"

What happened? You got distracted. You got comfortable. You achieved your objective (you got the one you loved), and then you started looking around. You took your eyes off the goal.

You left your first love. It happens all the time.

It happens in countries when they forget that it's in God they're supposed to trust. It happens in companies when they lose sight of why they were started in the first place. It happens in marriages when one or both partners start checking out other options. It happens in churches—and to Christians—when they swap out the pure love of Jesus Christ for some other thing.

It's dangerous to leave your first love. You do all kinds of damage to yourself and others. Sometimes that damage can never be repaired. A study of Scripture and history tells us that the church in Ephesus lost an amazing opportunity—forever.

ASIA'S FRONT DOOR

The church in Ephesus was positioned for greatness. But one day something went wrong, and the opportunity they had been given to impact the world for Jesus Christ just slipped away.

Ephesus was a tremendous city. In Bible times it probably had half a million people in the city proper. That was a large city back then. Ephesus had half as many people as Rome did, if that gives you any idea. (And if they had half the traffic we've got in Seattle, it would *still* take them an hour to get to work.)

The city had one of those half-circle amphitheaters carved into the hillside, which was large enough to seat twenty-five thousand people. Not bad considering Fenway Park only holds thirty-four thousand. (It's kind of funny to think that part of that two-thousand-year-old stadium in Ephesus is still standing, while Seattle's Kingdome—built on March 27, 1976—was so ancient that they had to implode it.) That was the stadium to which the Ephesians dragged Paul's friends in the riot in Acts 19. For two hours twenty-five thousand people shouted, "Great is Artemis of the Ephesians! Great is Artemis of the Ephesians!" You know, as a pro football player I've had twice that many people shouting bad things at me for two or three hours, and I can tell you that it's something you don't want to try.

Ephesus was the most important city of Asia Minor. It wasn't the capital; Pergamum was. But Ephesus was so influential that the Roman governor moved his digs over from Pergamum to Ephesus. Any dignitary to enter Asia Minor had to first come through Ephesus, regardless of where he was going. Four major trade routes converged at the seaport in Ephesus. It was the gateway to Asia Minor.

How important, then, do you think the *church* at Ephesus might have been, hmm?

How *strategic* was it for them to be located at the gateway to Asia?

How crucial was it for them to keep their lamps lit and held high? Think about that.

Ephesus was not only big and influential; it was also famous. It boasted one of the seven wonders of the ancient world, the Temple of Artemis. This thing was awesome. Check out what Philon of Byzantium, an ancient inventor, wrote:

> I have seen the walls and Hanging Gardens of ancient Babylon, the statue of Olympian Zeus, the Colossus of Rhodes, the mighty work of the high Pyramids, and the tomb of Mausolus. But when I saw the temple at Ephesus rising to the clouds, all these other wonders were put in the shade.[1]

No wonder the Ephesians got worked up when Paul began teaching that Artemis was no true god. Their entire identity was bound up in the worship of this goddess, whom you might also recognize as Diana, the goddess of sex. This was more than a religion—it was an industry! They had temple prostitutes, they had eunuchs, they had priests, and they had silversmiths making shrines and trinkets and little goddesses for the road. I don't know if they had Diana bumper stickers or mud flaps, but they had just about everything else. As the city official said in Acts 19, "Men of Ephesus, doesn't all the world know that the city of Ephesus is the guardian of the temple of the great Artemis and of her image, which fell from heaven?"

The image that "fell from heaven" was probably a meteorite. And if you dimmed the lights and squinted at it real hard, it might've looked a little like a female form with lots of…well, lots of qualities that would make her attractive as a sex goddess, if you follow me.

The Ephesians had so much invested in what they had built and the system they had going and the status of that system that they couldn't break away. They couldn't even think about deserting Artemis to worship another god.

People can be like that, too. Sometimes a person can put so much effort into a way of life that he can't turn away from it. He feels locked in by his financial obligations, by his emotions, by his relationships, by his tattoos or memberships or reputation or history. So even if he believes that his way is wrong and that Jesus Christ is right for him, he has invested too much to quit.

Don't be like that. What's it going to help you on the last day if you've been true to your old way of life and haven't followed Jesus? You don't get points for being loyal to what you knew was wrong. Have the guts to do the right thing no matter what it costs. I promise that it'll ultimately cost you less than if you don't.

So standing for Christ in Ephesus was not the most politically correct thing to do. But despite the tremendous religious persecution in Ephesus, God was doing great works in that bustling city. Paul spent three whole years there laying out the gospel, preaching and teaching his heart out, and building the Ephesian church. You can imagine the spiritual war that was going on: Paul's handkerchiefs were healing sick people, and Sceva's seven sons got whupped by a demon-possessed man for calling on the name of Jesus without faith. The church was growing in numbers and boldness. It was all leading up to that big riot Luke described in Acts 19.

When Paul left, he had Timothy stay behind to continue fighting the good fight. Later still, the apostle John came and set up shop there, devoting the latter part of his life to work in the city. Why? Because everyone understood the church's potential in that place. They all knew that Ephesus could become a huge influence for the church of Jesus Christ, not just in Asia Minor but all over the world. To put it in sports terminology, Ephesus was like a number one draft pick. Possibly no other church had greater potential. No other city outside Jerusalem got the kind of high-powered attention from the pillars of the early church. Ephesus was crucial, a portal to Asia. It was essential that the church there be living and effective.

By the way, you're a portal, too. Have you ever thought about that?

God has positioned you right where He wants you. If you are a Christian, your life is like a gateway, showing the folks around you what Christianity is all about.

For a while the church in Ephesus prospered. It was a beacon of truth, a fortress of faith, a city of light, an artesian well of pure Christian love. We've got Philadelphia, the city of brotherly love, coming up later in the book, but at that time no other city had anything on Ephesus.

"I KNOW YOUR WORKS"

While Paul was in a Roman prison he wrote to his beloved disciples in Ephesus. And as he did, one primary characteristic of that church kept coming to his mind.

Love.

Throughout the book of Ephesians, Paul emphasizes how the church of Ephesus was such a loving church of God. He talks about it in 1:15, he talks about it in 3:17–19, and he talks about it again in 6:23.

The Ephesian church didn't stop doing well after Paul was martyred, either. Paul wrote his love letter to them around A.D. 60, but when John received his revelation on the island of Patmos—probably sometime around A.D. 90—the church was still doing great things. Listen to the words of Jesus:

> "To the angel of the church of Ephesus write, 'These things says He who holds the seven stars in His right hand, who walks in the midst of the seven golden lampstands: "I know your works, your labor, your patience, and that you cannot bear those who are evil. And you have tested those who say they are apostles and are not, and have found them liars; and you have persevered and have patience, and have labored for My name's sake and have not become weary.""" (Revelation 2:1–3)

Wow! I'd say that was a pretty good report card. Wouldn't you want Jesus to say that about your church? Wouldn't you want Him to say that about *you*?

Hustle and muscle

He said He knew their works and their labor. "You are past just working for Me, Ephesus. You're beyond just haphazardly serving Me. Oh, no, you *labor* for Me. You get your back under it, Ephesus." Wouldn't you be excited to be in a church like that? Oh man, nobody had to scrounge for Sunday school teachers, nursery workers, or guys to volunteer for Saturday cleanup day. This church flat knew how to *work*. If you put a need in the bulletin, it got done!

Patience with people, none for evil

He also said He knew their patience. The particular Greek word Jesus selected here is usually used to describe patience in dealing with difficult people.

Is that what Jesus would say about you? Would He praise you for your patience with people that are hard to get along with? Ooh, we don't want to go there, do we? Patience in the grocery line? Patience on the expressway? Forget it.

Jesus also acknowledged that the Ephesian church could not bear with those who were evil. They didn't put up with evil people; they flushed 'em. As Paul once said, "Bad company corrupts good morals." The Ephesians had this under control.

Are you getting excited about the First Church of Ephesus yet? Are you ready to transfer your membership there? Are you surfing the cable channels to see if their services are on TV? Hang on, it gets better.

Defenders of the truth

The Lord tells them, "And you have tested those who say they are apostles and are not, and have found them liars." In other words: "You know hermeneutics, you know homiletics, you know Christology, your doctrine is watertight, you can break down the Scriptures with the best of them, and when someone is wrong, you can *prove* it."

Amen! Now *I'm* ready to go join this church. Come on, let's go. Just think what the folks sitting in their Ephesian pews thought when they heard this letter from Jesus Christ Himself. "I *know* your labor; I *know* your patience; I *love* how you handle the truth." I think I'd be riding pretty high if I heard that about my church.

Jesus goes on to say, "[You] have labored for My name's sake and have not become weary" (2:3). The Lord is saying, "Great job! When things got rough and people said you were intolerant and narrow-minded, you stood your ground and didn't compromise a single inch. Way to go, Ephesians."

Hating sin

But there's even more. The Lord tells them, "You have this in your favor: You hate the practices of the Nicolaitans, which I also hate" (Revelation 2:6, NIV).

Hating isn't a hate crime when you hate what the Lord Himself hates. Hate really is a "family value" when you hate sin with all your heart and soul. The world always wants to remind believers that Jesus is "loving and accepting and tolerant." But from the Lord's own mouth we hear of His complete hatred for the practices of a group of so-called believers that was leading His people astray. He tells the Ephesians, "You also hate the same deed I hate, and that is to your credit."

Okay, who were these Nicolaitans? They were smokers, right? No, that would be the Nicotinians—different group. We don't really know who the Nicolaitans were. Some scholars think they were followers of Nicholas, one of the deacons of Acts 5, 6, and 7. They think he got weird on everybody and led a bunch of the faithful into rack and ruin.

One thing we do know: the Nicolaitans were promiscuous. The Nicolaitans were Gnostics, folks who believed that you needed to keep your soul right, but as for what you did with your body…well, God understood. "I can get my heart and soul right, no problem. But to keep from having sex if I'm not married—well, that's just too much."

Let me tell you a secret. God says, "I hate promiscuity." You get it? Jesus said, "I like what you're doing, Ephesians. You stand against those who want to go out and have sex with anyone to whom they're not married." God does not wink at sexual sin and say, "Well, boys will be boys and girls will be girls." He *hates* it. So if you're having sex with someone that's not your husband or your wife, you'd better cut it out. *Fast.*

BUT…

So this church was a growing concern. It was the most truth-speaking, people-enduring, false-teacher-fighting, laboring-for-God church around. The church was growing; the city was taking notice; people's lives were being changed.

But…
The Head of the church had something against them.

"Nevertheless I have this against you, that you have left your first love. Remember therefore from where you have fallen; repent and do the first works, or else I will come to you quickly and remove your lampstand from its place—unless you repent.... He who has an ear, let him hear what the Spirit says to the churches." (Revelation 2:4–5, 7)

Jesus was saying, "Ephesus, you do a lot of things right, but I'm telling you, I've got something against you."

How can that be? You mean to tell me that Jesus found fault with a church *like that?* How could Jesus Christ say He had a problem with you when you were doing all of those kinds of things? What in the world could make Christ upset with a believer or a church like that one?

"You have left your first love."

Some people come to this verse and say the Ephesians had *lost* their first love. But that's wrong. They didn't lose it; they *left* it. The word means to forsake, abandon, neglect, put away. Their first love was still there, but they had left it behind and gone looking for greener pastures.

How many husbands abandon their wives? How many fathers abandon their families and run off with other women? I'm telling you, American men are going to receive terrible judgment from God because so many of them have left their families.

Women haven't been much better. Wives abandon husbands and children. Mothers abandon babies in hospitals or dumpsters or bus station restrooms. What kind of judgment do you think a woman who abandons the baby God put in her arms will receive? What kind of judgment when she aborts the baby God put in her womb?

The Ephesians had left their first love. They'd latched onto something secondary, something good but certainly not best. Be careful,

Christian! This can happen to you. *Anything that brings you greater satisfaction than God* is capable of stealing your first love. That can be another person, a possession, or an activity.

What or who was supposed to be their first love? Jesus Christ—who else?

How did it happen? How did they leave what their hearts used to hold most dear? Innocently. S-l-o-w-l-y. While they were doing lots and lots of "good things." I've seen it happen to churches and marriages and individuals time and time again.

Here's how I believe it went: While the Ephesians were busy enduring difficult people and shining their lights in that dark city and worshiping the Lord, the Nicolaitans sprang up. False teachers spreading heresy—but one that sounded so right, so "biblical."

The lies that most effectively poison the church are those that can heap up Scriptures to support their heresy. That's how Christian Science survives. That's how name-it-'n'-claim-it preachers survive. Throwing in a few Bible verses is how Jehovah's Witnesses and Mormons survive. That's how the David Koreshes of the world draw their followers. They dress their heretical ideas in Bible clothes. If the devil himself used Scripture when he tempted Jesus, why should we think less skilled liars wouldn't as well?

So I believe that the Nicolaitans came in and started talking up grace. Nice word, isn't it? It kind of rolls off the tongue. It sounds so pleasing, so nice, so religious. Grace is sufficient for everything, they said. Grace abounds where sin increases. Grace covers it all, amen? God's grace is greater than the vilest sin. Maybe they even used Paul's own words from his letter to the Ephesians: "For by grace you have been saved through faith, and that not of yourselves; it is the gift of God, not of works, lest anyone should boast" (Ephesians 2:8–9).

Sounds good, doesn't it? We would agree. "I'm there, brother! Preach it!" But what happens when you concentrate on grace and forget about works and responsibility and the pursuit of holiness? You get an unbalanced cart, my friend, and it's never long before an unbalanced cart dumps over.

You see, the Nicolaitans may have been handing out tracts about God's grace, but you had to read the fine print very carefully. When you read the fine print, you came to see that all their talk about grace was used to justify their wild sex parties. "Hey, grace covers everything, right? All things are permissible, right? God made the human body, didn't He? He made sex, and we're all believers here, so what's the problem?" How much do you think this heresy would appeal to folks in the city of the sex goddess?

What do you think the Christians there did? Did they cave in? Did they just lie down to the prevailing culture and become milquetoast? No sir! The Ephesian church did what was right. When they found out what the Nicolaitans were really about, the church took action. They made their stand on the truth of Jesus Christ and called those false teachers down.

Now—stay with me—I think this heresy was probably gaining popularity with the people who sought God but wanted to continue their worship of Artemis. They thought they'd found a way to keep their sex parties and follow Jesus, too.

Don't get too fat and happy, now. Don't start pointing your finger at *those people,* because the rest of us do the same kinds of things. We want to follow Jesus with part of our hearts, but with the rest we want to follow our own desires. Uh-oh! Have I gone from preachin' to meddlin'?

God hates *anything* that comes before Him in the number one spot in your heart. "You shall have no other gods before Me," He says. Not your job, not your house, not your reputation, not your old habits, and especially not your money. None of them.

I think the Ephesian Christians wanted to distance themselves from the heresy of those sex-crazed Nicolaitans. They wanted to appear to the people of Ephesus as something set apart from those compromisers. They wanted to act differently, talk differently, and worship differently. When they met for church, they probably steered away from anything that sounded like what the Nicolaitans would teach.

What was the result?

You guessed it.

A cart imbalanced on the *other* side.

In all likelihood they became a church that leaned so far from the grace-is-license crowd that the other extreme took over: too much emphasis on works, responsibility, and an external pursuit of holiness—a.k.a. *legalism*. In their effort to avoid Nicolaitanville, they ended up in Pharisee City.

"You have left your first love," said the Bridegroom. "You're holding to truth and exposing heretics and persevering, but your hearts have turned to stone. You've left your fervent love for Me and have turned into shriveled-up, freeze-dried finger-pointers—and *that's* what I have against you."

Know anybody like this? Anybody who should get an A for doctrine but an F-minus for mercy? Are *you* like this? To distance yourself from a friend's adultery, have you hardened your heart against that friend? In your passion to spot error in the church, have you turned into a cold-hearted condemner? Remember what James says: "Judgment without mercy will be shown to anyone who has not been merciful" (2:13, NIV).

Ephesus dropped the ball.

They were in the red zone with a first and ten on their opponents' nine-yard line, and they fumbled the snap.

God had positioned them for greatness, and they blew it big time. Not for lack of trying, but for lack of loving. So what happened as a result? A unique opportunity slipped away, *never to return*. They were strategically placed to show what Christianity was supposed to look like. They were the gateway to Asia, the portal to the Roman Empire. If they had stayed on track, I truly believe our world would be different today. I believe that the map of Christian nations would look very, very different.

God has positioned you for greatness, too, even if it doesn't look that way to you. No one else on God's green earth has the relationships, the experiences, the personality, or the opportunities that you have right now. *No one!* What you have is absolutely unique in this world and will *never* be duplicated. No one else will be given the opportunities in life that you have. What would happen if you were to drop the ball in your Christian life? What would happen if you were to abdicate the responsibility God has given you right there in that home, with that family, in that city, in this day and time?

If this is you, don't give up! If you've been a lousy gateway to Christ for the people closest to you, hang on. Jesus always brings hope to His children. No matter how far you've fallen, you're never so far gone that He can't pull you back to the victory road.

A SAD STATE OF AFFAIRS

"I just don't love him anymore."

We hear it all the time, don't we?

"I just don't have the same feelings for him anymore."

"The fire has gone out of our marriage."

"After the kids were born she gained all that weight—she just doesn't look good anymore. I'm outta here."

That's how people talk about leaving their first love when it's in a marriage. What do they say when they leave Jesus, the one who is supposed to be their ultimate first love? It might sound something like this....

"I just don't get as much out of church these days."

"You know, it's so hard to find time to read my Bible."

"There always seems to be something I need to do at home Sunday mornings."

One guy said, "I can get just as much out of church being at home listening to TV and tapes and speakers as going to the institution of the church."

Really? Just try that same argument in your marriage, and see how well it goes over. Tell your husband or wife, "I can get just as much out of watching a video of you!" See how quickly you'll be in my office, or in the emergency room!

Remember when you received your first love letter from that fellow or that girl? You could read it ten or fifteen times, no problem. Now you have a hard time getting in the Word. Why? Because you've left your first love. God doesn't like it, because when you leave your first love it's easy to compromise. When you leave your first love, anything else is fair game. When you leave your first love, there's no telling what you'll do.

ACTION PLAN

A believer's days may become very dark, and a believer's nights may seem to stretch on and on sometimes, but Jesus never leaves His children without hope. It was true for all seven churches Jesus spoke to in Revelation. It's true for you, too.

Look at how the Bridegroom approached His bride. He started with encouragement: "I know your works."

We need encouragement today, amen? We're starved for encouragement. Wives, your husbands are not any stronger than how you treat them at home. A man can put up with a lot of things out in the world, he can be beat up a great deal, but one thing he can't stand is to not be respected and encouraged by the woman he said he's going to spend the rest of his life with.

Husbands, your wives need your attention, your tenderness, your special care as much as your lawns need water. If you withdraw your love and become preoccupied with your own pursuits, they'll begin to dry up inside. The life will flow right out of them—and you will be held responsible for that before God. The command of Scripture is for husbands to love their wives…and that means pouring out your lives on their behalf, doing whatever it takes to encourage their hearts.

Jesus encouraged His children. And then He laid out the truth—"I have something against you." Finally, He told them what to do to get right with Him. This is a great pattern for dealing with brothers and sisters in the Lord who are on the wrong path. Start with the good, lay out the truth, and then help them back on the high road.

You want to get back to your first love? You want to return to the way things were back in the day when you first accepted Jesus Christ as your Savior? Guess what? Jesus has a three-step plan for you and me to get back to esteeming Him as first love: remember, repent, restart.

Check it out.

REMEMBER

"Remember therefore from where you have fallen."

In other words, you say, "Where was I, where am I now, and how in the world did I get *here?*" I've seen football players take a smack alongside the head and forget just about everything they ever knew.

Back in the days when I played middle linebacker for the Dallas Cowboys, we'd always get pretty jacked for our games with the Oakland Raiders. Our defense knew very well that the Raiders liked to run the sweep. It was no big secret—everybody understood they'd keep on running that student-body-right maneuver (and keep on getting first downs) until some defense found a way to stop 'em, which not many teams did in those days.

I decided that the way to stuff that play was by the direct approach. I would crash full speed into their blockers, disrupt the play, and let someone else nail the ballcarrier. So on one particular play I got a lightning start and went charging full bore into that advance wave of silver and black. But just as I approached the crest of that wave, the sea parted and the blockers sheered off, left and right. I ran straight into the back, who was also running as fast as *he* could. We went helmet to helmet. He went one way, I went another, and the ball went who knows where. It must have looked pretty cool, real highlight stuff. That Raider was out cold, and so was I; I just didn't know it yet. I jumped to my feet, pumped my fist in the air, yelled into the lights, then trotted back to the huddle.

For some reason the guys in the huddle started hassling me. "Get outta here! Beat it!"

Puzzled, I said, "What's wrong wich you? I creamed that guy. I killed him." Though I didn't know it, Coach Landry was yelling from the sideline, "Get him outta there! Get him off the field!"

The problem was this: I was a lonely Cowboy right in the middle of the Oakland Raider huddle! I didn't know who I was, and I didn't know who I played for. In fact, I wasn't even conscious. The guys had to fill me in on the details later than night.

The Lord says, "Sit down on that bench, and do some remembering. You've taken a big fall. Remember from where you have fallen. Remember how you got to this point. Remember your first love. Remember how you were with Me. When you get back into fellowship with Me, all the things that are bothering you right now will just fall away in importance. Remember what it was like when we walked together as Bridegroom and bride, Lover and beloved. *Remember.*"

Do you remember how sweet it was when you first came to Christ? You couldn't wait to get to church. Every word the preacher said was sweet—and the harder-hitting the truth, the better. Remember? You got into God's Word and were just blown away by what you read. You wanted to open your window and shout out the things you were learning. How could the earth hold itself together when words like that had been spoken? Remember? The Holy Spirit was your constant companion, your silent advisor, and that still, small voice in the night. Remember?

Come on back to Me, Jesus says, standing there with arms held wide, with pierced hands opened to you. Come on back to My love, and remember the way it used to be. It can be that way again.

REPENT

What did He say? *Repent.* He didn't say, "Think about it." He didn't say, "Kind of change." He said, "Repent." R-E-P-E-N-T. It's close to R-E-S-P-E-C-T. You've got to respect God and love Him and turn around 180 degrees.

The bottom line is that you can't get your first love back if you don't truly repent. I'm sorry to say that we don't have much repentance going on in the church today. Very little, in fact. But if you want to be different, if you want to walk with Christ like you did in the first days, repent. Say, "I'm not going to let myself get tripped up by that troublesome sin anymore—not for a week, not for a month, not for a year. I repent!"

RESTART

I saw so many green kids come into pro football. They thought they were *bad* because they had all this natural talent. Their drawers at home were stuffed with press clippings, and all their lives coaches had been telling them how great they were. So when they got into the pros they thought they could get by on raw talent alone. They thought other teams would read the scouting reports, believe the hype, and go belly up. Not in the NFL, my friend.

The players who ended up achieving the most in the NFL were not necessarily the most talented guys. Plenty of players with more talent ended up being cut by the end of training camp. Why? The ones who rose to the top were committed, they were coachable—and they never strayed from the basics: footwork, tackling, blocking, fitness, concentration.

If you want to return to your first love, you've got to get back to the basics: love for God, study of His Word, fellowship with believers, shining light in the darkness, and prayer—both talking and listening.

Love is a decision, amen? It's a commitment. It has nothing to do with emotions. Emotions *follow* obedience. Obedience is the bandleader marching out onto the field; emotions are the band, coming along behind with the cymbals crashing and the horns blaring. If you want to return to your first love, make a free-will decision and start moving in the right direction. Sure, God will give you the power to do it—but only after you take the first step! God convinces your heart; you convince your volition. Start today by doing the things you used to do when you first became a believer.

OR ELSE WHAT?

"Or else I will come to you quickly and remove your lampstand from its place—unless you repent." (Revelation 2:5)

Jesus, the head of the church, said that unless they remembered, repented, and restarted, He was going to remove their lampstand—remove their church.

Sadly, that's just what happened to Ephesus. Eventually the light from their lamp flickered and faded away, leaving the gateway to Asia Minor in terrible darkness.

And isn't that what He also warns the church about today?

Isn't that what He says to you and me?

"I will remove your power. I will remove what you used to be. I will remove how you used to affect people. I will remove your light out of the community and out of society."

And do you know what's happening to churches today? They are dying. Churches are dying. Denominations are dying. Some of them are already dead; they're just too lazy to fall over. Many Christians are the same way: They're still doing legalistic stuff, still doing so much of what the Bible says, but God has removed His power from them.

How sad! Don't be like that. Come on back to your first love.

OVERCOMING

"To him who overcomes I will give to eat from the tree of life, which is in the midst of the Paradise of God." (Revelation 2:7)

Throughout the seven letters Jesus holds out a blessing to the over-comer. But I'm so sick of hearing people misinterpret His meaning that I'm going to settle it right here.

It seems like a lot of people want to make this into a salvation issue. "You see?" they say. "If you don't overcome, you'll lose your salvation."

No, no, no, no. And may I say it one more time? *No.*

What He's saying is that those in God have overcome the world, and if you are in Christ, you automatically have overcome. And if you have automatically overcome, you automatically have Christ. If you automatically have Christ, you automatically have eternal life.

Still with me? If you automatically have eternal life, you're going to be living in the paradise of God, which is moved from the bosom of Abraham and is now in the presence of God. It is eternal life; it is heaven. If you are a true believer, you *have* overcome, and you *will* eat with God in heaven. That's what it's saying.

Before we leave this subject, let's check in one more time with the Lord of the church. What did He say about the salvation He would provide on the cross?

"Most assuredly, I say to you, he who hears My word and believes in Him who sent Me has everlasting life, and shall not come into judgment, but has passed from death into life." (John 5:24)

Once you have passed from death into life you *have* overcome, amen?

COME ON HOME

My brother or sister, the lover of your soul wants you back. He's the father in the story of the Prodigal Son: He never left. He's still there, waiting and watching for your return.

Don't sit there all depressed about how you've faltered, failed, and fallen. Get up and get moving. Get off the bench and back in the game. Remember how it once was when you were new in Christ and life was so sweet? It can be that way again! And even better.

There are no reasons why Christians should be miserable. None. I don't care what is going on; I don't care how difficult it is; I don't care what your excuses are. If you are miserable and let things get you down over and over for days and days, months and months, years and years, you are living in sin and need to repent of it. You need to do what it takes to walk with God.

Now did I say be blind to the truth? Pretend that there is no problem? No, I did not say that. God should be your first love, and if God is your first love, *nothing* can override His promises.

Not even the loss of a loved one.

Not even disease in a child.

Not even the rejection of a mate.

Emotions, yes; defeat, no. That's how I have chosen to live before God.

We have no business letting the world get us down. When I start feeling down, I turn to the last chapter of the book of Revelation. There is no way that I can ever, *ever* stay down when I have read that last chapter. I don't care how bad it is today—He's coming back, He's coming soon, and WE WIN!

Is your soul dry? Remember how it was when you first walked with your Savior. Have you become a judgmental finger-pointer? Repent and, by the grace of God, quit it. Have you become distracted by other things—good activities and responsibilities and relationships and opportunities? Restart. Do the first things.

Have you given your heart to anything besides the Lord Jesus Christ? If so, go running back to Him. Quick—before He removes the lampstand from your life. He won't remove His salvation from you, but He will remove the power, the ministry, the blessing—the strategic opportunities He gave you when He positioned you for greatness.

Make Jesus Christ your first love, and never leave Him again.

1. http://unmuseum.mus.pa.us/ephesus.htm

CHAPTER THREE

Smyrna:

FEELIN' THE HEAT

I've got some bad news, some good news, and some more bad news. Are you ready?

The bad news

The first bad news is this: God sometimes allows His children to suffer as part of His perfect plan for their lives. In fact, you might even say that the more He loves them and the more He wants to use them, the more they're going to suffer. Have I encouraged you yet? God said this to Ananias about Saul of Tarsus:

> "Go, for he is a chosen vessel of Mine to bear My name before Gentiles, kings, and the children of Israel. For I will show him how many things he must suffer for My name's sake." (Acts 9:15–16)

The Bible, if we read it right, shows us in no uncertain terms that God allows the righteous to suffer. That means *you* are going to suffer, too. You don't have to worry about it; you don't even have to think about it. It's going to happen.

If Jesus Christ, the perfect Son of God, learned obedience by the things He suffered (Hebrews 5:8), and if He suffered most when He performed His highest act of obedience to God, what makes us think we're going to get out of it?

Are you suffering greatly, even though you know your heart is right before God? Praise God—you're right on schedule! It means He's got something amazing for you to do. The suffering is coming because He has to get you in shape. Rejoice! You're on His select squad, the Elite Elect. You're on the same team with Joseph, Daniel, Jeremiah, Job, John the Baptist, Stephen, and Paul. That sounds like a dream team!

Who said that was bad news? That sounds like good news to me. But it doesn't *feel* good while the suffering is happening. That's the first bad news: God allows His kids to go through seasons of suffering.

The good news

The good news is that nothing and no one can touch you without God's permission. Flip the book over and look at my gorgeous face smiling at you. Do you realize you are looking at he who is invincible? I need a big *S* on my chest! SuperHutch! I'm unbeatable, unshakable, indestructible, and unstoppable. Nobody in the world can touch me...until God says it's time for me to go.

You can try to get rid of me if you want to, but you won't be able to do it. You can run over me with an eighteen-wheeler truck eighteen times, and I'll still be around if God wants me to be. I may not be able to walk, see, or talk, but you can't take my life. Why? Because I'm *invincible* as long as He who holds the keys to death in His hands holds the keys to my life.

That's the end of the good news. Uh-oh, uh-oh. More bad news coming.

More bad news

Nothing can touch me unless God gives His permission—that's good. But the flip side of that is that God does give His permission!

Thanks a lot, God! I thought You were my friend!

"Hutch?"

"Yes, God?"

"I thought you wanted to be on My A team. I thought you wanted to walk with Me on the high road. I thought you wanted to be on the Elite Elect."

"I do, I do."

"Then just hush up about this suffering. Just hush now. I'm here, and I know all about it. I was before *before* and I will be after *after*. Nothing is coming your way that I don't know about. Be quiet, quit talking. That's been your biggest problem in our relationship, Hutch. You talk so much that you can't hear *Me* when I speak. Just hush now and let Me do My work."

God's children suffer because God gives His permission for it to happen. Like it or not, God's favorite tool for making you and me Christlike is the power sander of suffering.

JUST ASK SMYRNA

Of the seven churches Jesus dictates letters to in Revelation 2 and 3, Smyrna is the one that experiences the fiercest persecution. Take a look:

> "And to the angel of the church in Smyrna write,
> 'These things says the First and the Last, who was dead, and came to life: "I know your works, tribulation, and poverty (but you are rich); and I know the blasphemy of those who say they are Jews and are not, but are a synagogue of Satan. Do not fear any of those things which you are about to suffer. Indeed, the devil is about to throw some of you into prison, that you may be tested, and you will have tribulation ten days. Be faithful until death, and I will give you the crown of life. He who has an ear, let him hear what the Spirit says to the churches. He who overcomes shall not be hurt by the second death.""'
> (Revelation 2:8–11)

How would you like to get *that* letter in the mail? The devil's about to throw you into prison, so you'd better be faithful until death—wouldn't that look nice on a Hallmark card? Oh my. Return to sender.

But there's something missing from this letter.

Where's the rebuke?

When you read these seven letters, the aspect that occurs in every one—except this one—is what Jesus has against them. "You do this and that and the other thing well, but I have *this* against you…." Smyrna is the only church of the seven that doesn't receive a reprimand. Not so much as a hand slap.

Think about that for a minute. The ascended Christ comes with a message to seven churches, and six of the seven have some serious sin they need to deal with. But one of the seven doesn't. One church out of the whole group is doing everything right. And the Judge of the living and the dead, whose eyes see through to the motives of men's hearts, has not one word of correction for them.

How do you think Jesus felt about that church? I get the feeling that He was sweet on it. Well, wouldn't you be? I don't know about you, but I think Smyrna was to the risen Lord what John was to Jesus when He walked the earth. John was the disciple "whom Jesus loved," the "beloved" disciple. When the disciples gathered together at the Last Supper, it was John who leaned on Jesus' shoulder and whispered into His ear. Now we've got seven churches sitting around the table, and who's that reclining on Jesus' shoulder? Smyrna.

THE FIRST CITY OF ASIA

Smyrna was an unbelievable city. It was nicknamed "the city of life and strength." Though Ephesus and Pergamum fought for preeminence, Smyrna nevertheless called itself "the first city of Asia."

In one sense, it was. As far back as 195 B.C. Smyrna could see that Rome was coming on strong, so they built a temple in which the Romans could worship their pagan gods. In 23 B.C., because of its years of faithfulness to Rome, Smyrna was given the honor of building a temple to the Emperor Tiberius. As far as Rome was concerned, Smyrna might've been the first city of Asia.

Smyrna was a beautiful city. Another nickname for it was "the beauty of Asia." The word *smyrna* isn't just a name; it's actually a word—it means "myrrh," and it appears in the New Testament three times (Matthew 2:11; Mark 15:23; John 19:39). Smyrna was like a sweet fragrance because of its beauty and because of its bustling commerce, made possible by its superb natural harbor.

And right in the midst of a city that prided itself on Roman paganism was a little Christian church. Its members probably met in someone's house. How do you think the people of Smyrna, with all of their emperor-worship, felt about this church of people who rejected all the Roman gods as idols? Probably something like the Ephesians with their temple to Artemis felt about the Christians in their city.

It was not fun to be a Christian in Smyrna. Why? Because they stood in opposition to how the prevailing culture wanted to live. Aha! Doesn't that sound familiar?

Do you know that the Judeo-Christian religious system is the only thing standing in the way of the world doing whatever it wants to do? And because of that the world says we are making them feel guilty about what they are naturally inclined to do. Think about it. If the church was not involved, if religion was not around, if that code of morality wasn't lifted high, what would the world do?

Anything. Everything. No holds barred.

If you're the only one protesting that a child is spoiled when everyone else is saying, "That child is not spoiled; he just has a way of expressing himself that's different from everyone else," what is that child going to think about you?

Jesus Christ says, "They hated Me, and I was perfect." When it comes to you and me as a church, believe me, we will be disliked if we stand up for what's right. So why are we so taken aback when it happens?

When the church stands up like that in this world, there's going to be pressure, tribulation, trouble, and angry people unable to understand how a church that believes in a loving God could raise such a stink. Churches aren't suffering very much for that today because they're not standing up for that which is right.

Smyrna did and Smyrna got smoked.

THE ANGEL OF SMYRNA

Some Bible scholars believe that when Jesus tells John to write letters to the angels of the churches in Revelation 2–3, He's telling him to write to the *leaders* of those churches. To the shepherds.

I know that it's true! All along I've been telling my church that their pastor is an angel: "Hutch is just so angelic." So far nobody believes me. But look out—now I've got biblical proof!

Who was the leader of the church in Smyrna? A guy you may have heard of if you've poked around any in early church history. Polycarp. Sounds like some kind of geometric fish, doesn't it?

Polycarp was the real deal. He was a friend and disciple of John— the same John who wrote Revelation, the same John who reclined on Jesus' shoulder. At the time Revelation was written, Polycarp was probably no older than twenty-five, but he served the Lord faithfully for sixty more years. His writings help us know church history just after the events recorded in Acts.

Polycarp was martyred by the Romans when he was eighty-six. Why did they kill him? Because he wouldn't deny Christ and light incense to pagan gods.

I'm telling you that if you stand for Christ against the world's wicked desires, you're going to get in trouble. Just count on it, and don't be surprised when it happens.

I had a taste of this pressure during my (very short) career with the San Diego Chargers. At that time and with that coach we were expected to do certain, shall I say, unusual things if we wanted to stay on the team. Those activities went against my conscience as a follower of Christ. I told the coach, "There are some things I'm just not going to do because football doesn't mean a hill of beans to me compared to walking with Jesus."

Do you know what the coach told me? He said, "I've got to have players down here I can depend on. And I suppose if God told you to quit at some point, you'd just up and quit the team, wouldn't you?"

"At the drop of a hat," I replied. (You see how subtle and sensitive I was?)

"Well, son, we've just got to have commitment if we're going to win as a team."

I said, "As long as God tells me to stay here, you've got a great player. But if He says, 'Go,' well, then *hasta la vista,* baby. Because you don't pay my paycheck. You think it comes through this organization, but I've got another boss."

They traded me, Jack! Got me off that team. I was a "bad influence."

Isn't that the pressure of being a believer? There's nothing people in the world hate more than somebody telling them they shouldn't live to satisfy their lusts and urges.

FIGHT OR FLIGHT

I got traded to Seattle because of my stand for Christ.

Polycarp got killed.

The world killed Jesus Christ and Peter and James and Paul—and many, many others. Maybe the reason John wrote Revelation was because he was the only original disciple left alive! The others had all been martyred for their faith.

What would you do if you were told to deny Christ or die? What if you were forced to deny Christ or watch your children die? What's your price? How much torture could you endure before you broke down and gave them what they wanted? I've read stories about early Christians who rushed after the lions so they could die faster and be with Christ. Would I do that when the time came? I hope I would, but I have to admit that the thought gives me just a sliver of fear.

"Do not fear any of those things which you are about to suffer." That's what Jesus told the Christians in Smyrna. Their persecution wasn't coming from Jews, as it appeared, but from false Jews, members of the "synagogue of Satan," Jesus said. It was the devil himself who was opposing them. Not only that, but that Serpent was going to throw some of them into jail and press them even to death.

I think I'd be a tad bit afraid, wouldn't you?

But in the midst of this terrifying message about tribulation, prison, and death, there's just something reassuring in Jesus' words. Maybe it's this: If the devil's behind this suffering, then the Christians can *know* that Jesus is fighting for them. Talk about friends in high places! Jesus, the Mighty One, says, "I am part of this battle, so you have nothing to fear. I'm going to bash some heads in for you, so just relax."

"I KNOW"

When Jesus told the Christians in Smyrna to have no fear of the tribulations that were coming upon them, He gave them two all-important words, two words of power that would light their way through the darkest dungeons....

"I know."

Listen as He speaks those words to the suffering believers in Smyrna:

> "I know your works, tribulation, and poverty (but you are rich); and I know the blasphemy of those who say they are Jews and are not." (Revelation 2:9)

Your works? *I know them.*
Your tribulation? *I know it.*
Your poverty? *I know all about it.*
Your abuse? *My child, I know.*
Your persecution for My sake? *I know, I know, I know.*

One thing you'll never hear from Jesus Christ are the words, "I don't understand. I just don't know what you're going through. I may be God, but—I'm sorry—your situation's just beyond Me."

What did He say instead?

I know.

When you're hurting, *I know.* When you want to give up, *I know.* When you can't take it anymore, "I know all things about you. I know what's good for you. I know what you can bear and what you can't. I know where I'm going with you and what I'm doing in you. You're right on schedule. My child, I know!"

You may feel that you don't get recognized. You may feel that God isn't coming through on His part. You may say, "Look, I've given up so much for You, God, that I think it's time for You to start giving me a few of those blessings back." You may feel that no one understands. You may wonder, *Boy, is it worth it?*

What does God say? "I know your works."

Isn't that one of the most comforting things you have ever heard? Your heavenly Father knows what's happening with you. He hasn't overlooked a single thing. He knows those deep-down feelings you could never put into words. He knows those dreams and hopes and longings you've never whispered to a single soul.

Maybe you're lonely. Maybe you want to get married sometime soon, like yesterday. What does God say? "I know your loneliness." He knows. But keep this in mind, too: If He doesn't change your loneliness, it's because you *need* to be lonely. God knows that the best thing for you right now is for you to be lonely. Why? Because you and I have a tendency to trust in things besides God to remove our loneliness. "I know your loneliness, but until you can trust in Me and only Me to fill up that place in you that wants to be filled, I'm going to keep you lonely."

Maybe you're suffering pain or sickness or grief. Your beautiful Savior says, "I know your pain." That's the good news: He knows your pain. The bad news is that God says you *need* to hurt. Why? Because it's the only thing that's going to make you learn to trust in the One who has the soothing balm of Gilead. "I know when to allow you to get into difficulty, and I know when to let you out. I am God, and you are not. And I know what's best."

STAY PUT

God knows your situation. He knows all your fears and hurts. But He doesn't always take you out of them. No, sir. Your situation is for your sanctification and for God's glory. You are in this hard place because this is the way God has deemed it best for you to learn what He wants you to learn and to accomplish what He wants you to accomplish.

Look at the believers in Smyrna. He said He knew their works and their tribulations. But then He said, "Hang on, it's going to get a lot worse before it gets better. I'm not going to take you out of the hot seat yet. But don't worry: This will work out for your benefit."

> I know your works, tribulation, and poverty (but you are rich);
> and I know the blasphemy of those who say they are Jews and
> are not, but are a synagogue of Satan. Do not fear any of those
> things which you are about to suffer. Indeed, the devil is about
> to throw some of you into prison, that you may be tested, and
> you will have tribulation ten days. Be faithful until death, and
> I will give you the crown of life. (Revelation 2:9–10)

When we need comfort or help, the first thing we usually say is, "God, if only I had more money!" We think having more money will deliver us from the pain we're feeling. But that's not the way God usually works. When a church or a family is hurting like crazy and God knows they need some encouragement, He doesn't usually bring more money or immediately move them into a comfortable situation. (Sometimes I wish He would!)

What does He say instead? He says, "I know your works, tribulation, and poverty (but you are rich)" (Revelation 2:9).

That doesn't make sense, God. You say You know my poverty, but then You say I'm rich? What's up with that?

I think God is saying that we're not going to be protected from hurt all the time. But in the midst of that hurt and as a result of that hurt we're going to be a lot better off than if we'd never hurt at all.

When Jesus speaks, He speaks as the Alpha and the Omega, the First and the Last. He speaks as the Eternal One who is beyond calendars, beyond clocks, beyond time. He knows that although our years on earth may seem long, although our suffering may seem endless, our lives are only a heartbeat—the blink of an eye—alongside eternity.

What was waiting for Smyrna at the end of all the suffering? The crown of life. The overcomer's prize doesn't go to the bystander; it goes to the one who has paid the price to endure to the end in the midst of pain. If suffering is the pathway to special blessing from God, then maybe I'm not so sure I want out of it, after all.

If I could only make my knees stop knocking together.

OVERCOMING FEAR

We live in a world gripped by fear. Fear of being alone, fear of being hurt, fear of theft or violation. Fear of suffering, fear of death, fear of losing control. People barricade themselves inside their homes and pay thousands of dollars for security systems and concealed handgun permits. So many times the motivation behind what people in the world do is fear.

The sad thing is that fear is alive and well in *Christian* homes, too, isn't it?

We hold on to all the same fears the world holds on to. More decisions are made out of fear in Christian homes than out of faith. It's a sin. Fear*ful* means faith*less*—especially since we've been told by Jesus Christ not to fear the tribulations that are going to come. Why should we fear death when our afterlife is secure? Why should we fear those who can kill the body when we're allied with the One who can send the soul to hell?

I'm not sitting here pointing my finger at you. No, no. I struggle with fear myself.

In some things I'm fearless.

Stand for Jesus in the face of an angry world? You betcha.

Stand up for right when a brother's doing wrong? I'm there.

Fight for my children or my wife or my home? You know it.

But I do struggle with two main fears. And sometimes I set my eyes on those fears. They say confession is good for the soul but bad for the reputation. Well, I'm going to risk it. I'm going to confess my two greatest fears.

COULD WE JUST DRIVE?

I hate flying. Okay, you saw right through that statement, didn't you? "I hate flying" is just another way of saying I *fear* flying. One thing I know about God is that He will always make you face your fears. So guess what I have to do a lot? Fly.

I'm not afraid of falling. I don't know why everyone's afraid of that. Falling doesn't hurt—it's the sudden stop! I'm not afraid of dying when I fly. No. If I'm going to crash, I'd *rather* die. What I'm afraid of is being maimed and burned—and not dying. I'm afraid of being helpless and weak and horrible to look at. I'm afraid of scaring my kids and making my wife sick. As you'll see in a second, this fear feeds right into my second fear.

This flying thing is a constant struggle for me, a thorn in the flesh. Every time I have to climb into a plane, I've got to make sure I'm thinking about God and not the flight itself. I've got to make sure I'm trusting in Jesus to hold that heavy metal airplane in the air, not the pilot or Boeing or the laws of aerodynamics.

TAKING CARE OF BUSINESS

My second major fear is that of not being able to take care of things that are my responsibility. I fear not being able to provide for my family. I fear not being able to take care of the ministry God has given me. I fear not being able to look after all the people that are employed by and cared for through the church.

Sometimes I just don't have the money I need. People need things that take money, and I can't help them. Sometimes the church doesn't have the money it needs to pay salaries and take care of things that need to be paid for. Sometimes my kids need me or my wife needs me, and for whatever reason I just don't have the time I need to give them. It drives me nuts! I truly am afraid that I will be found guilty of not doing what I should be doing for the people who count on me.

This is a battle I have to fight all the time. I have to stay on top of this one and keep my eyes on the goal. Because if I let it go for just one full thought, I am defeated. I become miserable, mean, and cutting. In other words, I become just like anybody else in the world.

That's the power of fear in the lives of believers: It can make us just like lost people, ruled by fear. Fear has no place in the believer's heart—mine included—because Jesus Christ, who is "perfect love," is there—and perfect love casts out fear.

STEPS TO CONQUERING FEAR

I've developed a four-step plan to help me get past my own fears. I think it'll work for you, too.

The first step: Get your eyes repaired

Jesus said that the eye is the window to the soul:

> The lamp of the body is the eye. If therefore your eye is good, your whole body will be full of light. But if your eye is bad, your whole body will be full of darkness. If therefore the light that is in you is darkness, how great is that darkness! (Matthew 6:22–23)

How do you look at things? Are you pessimistic? Do you view life through the lens of fear? If you see things darkly and always see the glass as half-empty, you make those around you miserable. So long as you constantly focus on how bad things are you will never get out of your fear.

If your eyes are dark, I'll bet I could write down ten characteristics of what your family is like, because negativity has a tendency to bring everyone down. That's when most marriages break up—when both the husband and the wife are negative at the same time. Negativity's only power is to tear down. If you've got a double dose of darkness in your home, what's left but to destroy your family? Enough negativity will destroy any family, any church, and any nation.

Your only hope is to have eye surgery. You're pessimistic and afraid because you're looking to something unreliable to save you—namely, yourself. You know your limitations, yet you may be trusting in yourself to save the situation. Or maybe you're trusting in something else that is also fallible, like any other human or organization or machine or doubtful promise. If you want to get beyond your fear, there's only one way: by getting your eyes fixed—fixed, that is, on Jesus.

So make an appointment with the Great Physician. Submit yourself to His care. Go under the knife of His no-stitch procedure. When the bandages come off and your eyes are fixed on Jesus Christ, your soul will fill with light, and your fears will disappear.

Jesus is the Rock of Ages, the Mighty Fortress, the Lion of Judah, and the King of kings. He created the universe, parted the Red Sea, and rose from the dead. If you're looking to *Him* to manage your life, you will be singing worship songs, not funeral dirges.

Peter locked his gaze on Jesus and walked on water. When he took his eyes off Jesus and focused on the waves, he sank like a sandbag. Elisha's servant saw the Syrian army and was afraid. But Elisha performed eye surgery on him and he saw the army of God in mighty array surrounding the Syrians! You and I turn cowardly when we look at our problems and our limitations. But when we fix our eyes on what God *can* do, not on what we *can't* do, our fears will melt into confidence, and we'll go our way rejoicing. Hallelujah, what a Savior!

Make an appointment today.

The second step: Get rid of the fear of dying

God says that if you want to get rid of fear, you've got to get rid of your fear of dying. Hey, if you live long enough, you're gonna die anyway! One out of one people will face death—unless Jesus comes for us first. (When it comes to the Rapture of the church, I have no fear of flying. Aim me toward those clouds, and watch me launch!)

> Inasmuch then as the children have partaken of flesh and blood, He Himself likewise shared in the same, that through death He might destroy him who had the power of death, that is, the devil, and release those who through fear of death were all their lifetime subject to bondage. (Hebrews 2:14–15)

Did you see that? The fear of death leads to a lifetime of bondage. Is that how you're feeling—in bondage to your fears? Do you know someone like this? Lost people are in bondage to their fears. But that's all that can be expected of them—they need the liberation of Jesus. Christians, on the other hand, are supposed to be different. We're supposed to be set free, because where the Spirit of the Lord is there is freedom.

God says you will never get rid of your fear until you come to the realization that He is life, that in Him there is no death, and that to die physically is simply to be with Him. Oh, what emancipation, what freedom, what a life!

Take me, for example. I will stand up for God in any situation to any person. I don't care how big the church or organization is, if you are wrong, I'm in your face. I'm fearless before God. Because the worst thing they can do to me (which is also the best thing they can do to me) is put me to death. And what then? Well, then I'm on my way to my Father and my family collects a big insurance check!

Tell me, what can anyone do to me if I'm not afraid of dying? What can he threaten me with? What if I'm not afraid of losing my reputation? What if I'm not afraid of losing this church because I stand up? What is anyone going to threaten me with? If they say they're going to hurt me, I'd say, "Don't hurt me; *kill* me! Send me to my Savior!"

Now, if I can walk with God and do everything He asks me to do with that attitude, so can you. Settle in your heart that you're not afraid of dying, because inside you is the resurrection and the life. Your eternity is secure, and you're invincible on earth until it's your time to go. What's left to fear? Why not just go ahead and live for God to the max?

The third step: Realize that God is in control

If you're anything like me, you know that God *could* come through to take care of whatever it is you're afraid of, but you just don't know if He *will*. We're like Martha watching the horizon, waiting for Jesus to come running to save her brother. She has no doubt that Jesus has the power to save Lazarus. What blows her away is that He chooses not to arrive in time.

See, I want God to come through for me tomorrow. (I'd really like to have Him come through yesterday, but today or tomorrow will be okay.) But then it hits me that God is sovereign, which means He will not come through until He wants to. When I think about that, fear pops in real quick. But guess what? I've got a sovereign God and so do you. He may not come through tomorrow. Or the day after that. The question I have to ask myself is this: Can I be just as satisfied tomorrow as I am today if He doesn't come through?

Let's take another look at the Lord's words to the persecuted believers in Smyrna:

> "Do not fear.... You will have tribulation ten days. Be faithful until death, and I will give you the crown of life. He who has an ear, let him hear what the Spirit says to the churches. He who overcomes shall not be hurt by the second death." (Revelation 2:10a–11)

Jesus is in the house. He's in charge of what's happening to these Christians. There's a purpose for it, an end to it (signified by "ten days"), and a prize on the other side of it. They can put their fears to death by clinging to the certainty of His sovereignty.

By the way, so can you.

The fourth step: Confess the sin of fear

I could've listed this one first since none of the others will work if you don't do this one. If you truly want to get rid of your fear, you've got to see it as sin and deal with it as such. "If we confess our sins, He is faithful and just to forgive us our sins and to cleanse us from all unrighteousness" (1 John 1:9).

What is fear but unrighteousness? God says that if you confess your sins and forget to talk about your fear, He is faithful to wipe out your fear in your confession. Because as long as you've got open sin in your life, it is impossible for you to be fearless. As you'll see in just a minute, if you're fearful, it's impossible for you to be faithful.

Think about it: How can you stand up for Jesus Christ in the world when you know there's unconfessed sin in your life? Your soul is weak and your body fights against you. You can't rest and the sin eats you alive. To be fearless you must confess your sin and step out in faith.

I want you to do something for me right now. I want you to honestly look at yourself and name your fears. You know what they are. Go ahead and hold those things in your head. Now pray something like this:

God, I confess to You that I have allowed my fears to put me into bondage. I know I must now give them to You. Lord, please change my eyesight. I confess this as a sin and want to get rid of it. I acknowledge that You're in control, Father, and I choose to think on Your abilities rather than my limitations. And I know that I've got to learn to love You more, God, because Your perfect love casts out my fear. Lord, I thank You, for You are God. Amen.

FEARLESS MEANS FAITHFUL

You can't cling to fear and faith at the same time. I don't care who you are—you can't do it. You can't say, "I've got faith in God, and He's going to protect us, and everything's going to be all right through Him," and then go out and fear what the world says is going to happen.

Fear and faith are on opposite sides of a coin, and I've never yet seen a coin toss where you get heads *and* tails. They may have something to do with each other, but you will never see them both at the same time.

Now, you and I can't be fearful and faithful at the same time, but let me tell you something we can do: We can go back and forth real quick! *Flip! Flip! Flip!* I can sit here and say, "Man, I trust God, amen; God's going to come through," but by the time I take half a step I can be worried again. You can't have fear and faith at the same time, but, boy, can you make a quick transition.

The trick is that one is a natural impulse, and the other is a command. One is the result of trusting in something untrustworthy; the other is the result of trusting in Someone who can be trusted. One makes you weak, and the other makes you strong.

Jesus says, "If you do what I ask you to do, be fearless and faithful, you're going to be faithful unto death. Why? Because fear is not going to be what motivates you to make your decisions."

Set your eyes on the risen Christ and what He can do. Get rid of the fear of dying. Cling to His sovereignty. And confess the sin of fear. If you do, your fear will be transformed into faith.

HIS WAITING ARMS

God allows Christians to suffer. Not to discipline them for sin, not because He's unaware of their situation, and not because He's unable to deliver them from harm. No, Christians suffer because God uses suffering to perfect the image of His Son in His children. Satan is behind some of the suffering—as he was behind the Smyrna believers' suffering—but it is ultimately God who uses it to accomplish His purposes.

That sounds good, doesn't it? It's comforting to know. But if you're *in* the suffering, it may not seem like such a great idea. If you're being threatened or attacked or bullied for standing for Christ and His righteousness, all of this theology of suffering doesn't ease your distress at all.

That's when Jesus' words come to our rescue. "Don't fear the tribulation that's about to come upon you," He says, "even though it will be bad. Keep your eyes fixed on Me and stand up straight. I've got you covered. If you live, you will live to praise Me more. If you die, you will come to My waiting arms. Overcome, My child, and receive the crown of life."

CHAPTER FOUR

Pergamum:
IN THE SIFTER

A s I look at Scripture, it seems to me that Christians have two choices when it comes to living in this world. We're either going to walk with Christ and face at least some form of persecution and rejection, or we're going to knuckle under to the king of this world, the prince of dead air, Satan himself. Those are the only two choices we have as a church or as individual believers.

We're either going to do God's work, or we're going to do Satan's work.

This is competition; this is war. If you accept Jesus Christ as your Lord and Savior, you can expect opposition from the world. Why? Because the prince of this world—the one who owns this place—is Satan. That's why this earth is going to be destroyed. If God owned it, it wouldn't be destroyed. He owns you and me, so we're not going to be destroyed. But the earth and the lost are going down.

Satan knows he has lost the war, but you can bet he's going to raise a stink before he's finished. Remember the burning oil fields left by the Iraqis when they retreated from Kuwait? Same idea.

Satan is the enemy of God and God's children. Our struggle is not against flesh and blood, Paul reminded us, but against supernatural powers of evil. And never forget it: Satan *hates* Christians. He hates us because he knows he has lost. He's lost his place in Eden, he's lost his position as the greatest of all creatures, he's lost his war in heaven, and he knows the end of the story better than you and me. There's nothing left for him but to try to spoil the Victor's prize.

Right now he's pursuing a scorched-earth, scorched-soul strategy. If God wants to use Christians to do His work in the world, Satan will do all he can to prevent it. He'll deceive and seduce and bully and scare—anything he can do to keep God's people from doing God's work. He wants to keep you silent, on the sideline, mediocre. Let me tell you something: If you're not facing spiritual opposition in your life, it may be because the devil knows you're nothing to worry about!

IN THE SIFTER

Satan is the prince of this world. He's like a roaring lion that goes to and fro looking for whom he can devour. Anyone without the protection of God is in trouble if Satan comes after him. Lost people have no defense. None.

What about Christians, then? Do you think believers are immune to Satan's attacks, that we are somehow protected from his fury? Think again:

And the Lord said, "Simon, Simon! Indeed, Satan has asked for you, that he may sift you as wheat." (Luke 22:31)

Does that give you the willies, even just a little? God gives Satan the opportunity to chastise you and me, even as believers.

Satan is a sifter. He wants to sift every one of us. That doesn't sound like anything very nice, does it? Satan wants to shake you up so that all the good will be shaken out—so that the only thing left will be what's bad. That way you'll die lost or, if you're a Christian, you'll lose your witness and die as a poor servant of Christ. That's Satan's desire. That's his job. That's what lights his fire and floats his boat.

Which is why we shouldn't be surprised at *anything* a lost person will do. Walk into a church and open fire? Sure. Blow up a school? Sounds good. Steal the socks off an honest company? Why not? We also shouldn't be surprised when Satan's people self-destruct. They kill themselves. They sabotage their chances. They destroy their families. They blow their inheritance. Why? They're in the sifter.

I wish I could say that Christians were exempt from those behaviors, but I can't. Blow up an abortion clinic? Sure. Cheat on your spouse? Sounds good. Embezzle from the church? Why not? Christians in the sifter can be every bit as self-destructive as non-Christians. God is still sovereign; He still holds their destiny and their souls. But they are living like the world.

See, God allows Satan to sift us just like He allows suffering to come to His children. Why does He allow it? Because that's how we learn obedience and get formed into the image of His Son. God says, "I want Satan to put you in the sifting bowl. I want him to knock you back and forth and front and back. The testing of your faith produces endurance—and I want enduring saints!"

God has given Satan the job of sifting you. He's given him permission to loose his demons on your life. But this is not to harm you. God has a plan in mind, a desirable outcome. The result God wants to draw from Satan's sifting is this: You will be shaken until there is no bad left in you. All the bad will be sifted out.

Of course, Christians get to choose how they *respond*. Choosing is God's gift to us. When hard times come, when suffering comes, when the sifting comes, we can choose to fall on our knees or fall flat on our faces. We can turn to God for help, or we can turn to Him with clenched fist. (And I don't mean Black Power—I mean anger at God.) The outcome of the sifting is always up to you. What's left over after the sifting is determined by what's in there in the first place, at the core.

Satan is a sifter. If you're not being sifted now, it's coming. Count on it. But how you endure that sifting is up to you. I am ashamed that many believers give Satan the right to win in their lives when he has no right to any victory there. None. But you have to decide. You can choose at any moment to be an instrument of righteousness or an instrument of unrighteousness.

As for me and my house, we're going to march for God, and we're going to kick Satan all over the place as long as I confess my sins, yield to the control of God's Spirit, stay in His Word, and remain obedient to what I know.

That's when victory comes.

And take it from an old weekend warrior…victory is *always* sweet.

SATAN'S THRONE

The cities we've looked at so far have had some claim to fame. Ephesus was the gateway to Asia and de facto capital. Smyrna was the commercial center. Pergamum was the official capital of the Roman province of Asia, although the governor had moved his headquarters to Ephesus. More importantly, Pergamum was the religious center of Asia Minor.

Pergamum boasted an altar to Zeus that many believe to have been the throne of Satan referred to in Revelation 2:13. The artwork on this fantastic altar showed Zeus defeating snakelike giants. The snakes could be a reference to another god worshiped in Pergamum: Asclepius. Asclepius was the god of medicine. His symbol was the caduceus, the winged staff with two snakes wrapped around it (still the symbol of physicians today).

Pergamum possessed a famous hospital and school of medicine. Patients would come from far and wide to have the priests of Asclepius dream dreams. Apparently the answers to the patients' problems would sometimes be revealed to the priests as they slept. Besides temples to Zeus and Asclepius, Pergamum maintained worship centers for Dionysus, Athena, Apollo, Aphrodite, and three Roman emperors who were worshiped as gods. It was like a shopping mall of false gods. It was Satan's throne, all right.

As you might imagine, Christians weren't well represented on the chamber of commerce.

Funny, isn't it? You'd think that with such a diversity of gods Christianity would slip right in there with all the rest of 'em, wouldn't you? But it never works that way. Christians have the annoying tendency of calling all other gods false except the Christian God. The pagans in Pergamum exerted tremendous pressure on Christians to shut up, sign up, or drop dead. Scholars believe that the priests of Asclepius were the ones who martyred Antipas. No wonder the rest of the Christians kind of slunk away.

"And to the angel of the church in Pergamos write,

'These things says He who has the sharp two-edged sword: "I know your works, and where you dwell, where Satan's throne is. And you hold fast to My name, and did not deny My faith even in the days in which Antipas was My faithful martyr, who was killed among you, where Satan dwells. But I have a few things against you, because you have there those who hold the doctrine of Balaam, who taught Balak to put a stumbling block before the children of Israel, to eat things sacrificed to idols, and to commit sexual immorality. Thus you also have those who hold the doctrine of the Nicolaitans, which thing I hate. Repent, or else I will come to you quickly and will fight against them with the sword of My mouth.""" (Revelation 2:12–17)

Did you catch that? These Christians stood firm in the days when Antipas was going to the wall for Christ. But then they backed away from the truth and tolerated the doctrine of Balaam.

These believers were fickle. They would stand strong one day and the very next day say that a little bit of sin wouldn't hurt anything. Sound like anyone you know?

They'd had an example in this. The Jews in Pergamum had already caved. Many Jews lived in Pergamum. Maybe they even had a syna-gogue in the town. But most of the Jews were more or less assimilated with the Greeks—even to the extent of having Greek names. So there was precedent for compromise in Pergamum. The Christians knew they had better conform to pagan ways or die.

FAITHFUL WITNESS

The Bible doesn't tell us much about Antipas except that he was faith-ful and that he became a martyr. I don't know about you, but if God is going to write something on my tombstone, I can't think of anything better than, "Hutch—faithful witness and martyr." (Of course, as of right now I'd want them to write, "I *told* them I was sick." But that doesn't have the same effect spiritually, does it?)

I am absolutely amazed when I see what compromise will do to a church and to Christians. Look at this church in Pergamum. The believers here stood strong when they were being persecuted for their faith, even to the point of death for one of their members—maybe their leader. But when it came to the sensual sins of the smooth-talkin' Nicolaitans, they didn't stand at all.

Why not? It doesn't add up.

Will you let me describe how I think things might've gone on that fateful day in Pergamum? Let's take a minute and picture how it might've been when Antipas was martyred.

There's brave Antipas, dragged to the acropolis of the city, taken to the priests on the hill, brought to the temples of false gods, being threatened to deny Christ by burning incense to idols. The believers from church are there, too. They're shouting and pushing and praying like mad. They're getting pushed around by the people. The Jews are there, yelling with the pagans.

Antipas is brought before the altar of Zeus and given one last chance: Deny Christ or die. Praise God he stands firm. He looks those priests in the eye and says, "Though you slay me, yet I will worship the only true God, Jesus Christ—born of a virgin, crucified, buried, resurrected, and reigning on high!"

Off goes his head. The pagans shout in victory; the Christians wail in agony. The crowd disperses. The believers take Antipas's body to holy ground and bury it with many a prayer and song and tear.

Afterward they return to their homes and they think.

They think a lot.

They replay the event in their minds.

They have bad dreams.

The people of the city turn hostile eyes on them when they pass. In their minds they still see the priest raising Antipas's severed head in the air and shouting, "So will be the fate of anyone who does not worship the holy gods of Rome!"

Days pass. Weeks. They meet in secret now. They bar the door and post a guard. Their meetings are subdued, almost reluctant. Where is their victory? Where is their joy? Where is the sweet fellowship and sweeter worship they'd enjoyed when their brother Antipas had led them so boldly?

"But look where that got *him*," someone says. "Better to just lay low and pretend to worship the gods. We don't want to attract attention. Some of us have families. Do we really want them to come to the same end as Antipas?"

Some of the believers think this is wrong. They think it's a crime against God and against Antipas's memory to join the society of secret saints. But they don't have any wish to meet the chopping block, either. So they remain silent.

When the Nicolaitans arrive and begin teaching their doctrine of Christianity mixed with sexual promiscuity, no one says anything. The heresy grows quickly, finding little resistance. By the time anyone is offended enough to say anything it's too late. Nothing but a very public split can oust them now. Since nobody wants to attract attention, they just let it ride.

How'd I do? You think this sounds like how it might've gone down? Satan comes in with a one-two punch. First he uses intimidation to reduce the believers to silence. Then he uses temptation and compromise to seduce them into apathy. He's got both going on in Pergamum. What's the result? Christians sitting out the battle. And Satan humming his favorite tune.

GO FIGURE

Compromise doesn't make sense if you really think about it. How can you stand extremely strong in one aspect of your Christian life and totally submit to sin in another? This church at Pergamum stood strong in the face of persecution but then put up with the gross sin of the Nicolaitans. Are you scratching your head, too?

Now let me ask you a question. If you want to be a Christian and really walk with God, do people respect you more when you are consistent through all aspects of your life or when you are strong in some areas of your life and compromise in others? Olympic athletes who spend half their training time watching TV and eating Twinkies don't command much respect. It's the devoted person, the sold-out person—the consistent person—who becomes a champion.

Consistency helps convince those that are looking for a Savior. Inconsistency does major damage to Christianity and to your witness. Satan loves it, though. You're playing his song. How does that tune go? "There may be some compromisin' on the road to my horizon, but I'm goin' where the lights are shinin' on me!"

Compromise is his way.

He knows he can't have us, but boy can he give us opportunities to royally mess up our lives. The sad thing is that we often take him up on those opportunities. We think that if we drop our standards a little bit when we're with some of our unbelieving friends, we're going to somehow influence them and love them into the kingdom. Too bad, Jack. It doesn't work that way.

I was listening to some politicians recently. (There are only two evils in the world today: politicians and pastors. I chose the lesser of the two evils!) They were discussing the issue of abortion. They were so inconsistent it was ridiculous. They would say whatever they thought anyone wanted to hear—say one thing to this group to get their votes, say something else to another group to get theirs. Who cares about consistency? All that matters is the final vote count.

Do you know any Christians like that? Inconsistent as all get out? The believers in Pergamum were willing to go to the wall on one issue but could compromise like crazy on two or three others. I know some folks like that today.

I know Christians who won't go to a movie—"It is so ungodly to go to a movie!"—but then they turn around and curse each other out.

I know Christians who will debate you if you're off a point or two on your theology—and then drink you under the table after you get through discussing doctrine. They may even drink you under the table *while* you're discussing doctrine!

I know Christians who will do forty-five in a fifty-five-mile zone because they don't want to speed—"Oh, how ungodly it is to speed"—but then they'll sleep with someone that is not their husband or wife.

I know Christians who won't play the lottery. They won't even play bingo—"Only sinners do that gambling!"—but then they'll grab their newspapers and turn straight to their horoscopes: "Uh-oh. Bad day for me. Better stay inside."

I know Christians who will picket at the abortion clinic and then drive home with their New Age crystals hanging from their mirror—"Oh, pastor, I just love the way the sun sparkles through it." Uh-huh.

Don't come to me with your legalistic attitude if you're not going to be consistent, because the church should not be like Pergamum, it should be like Christ. If I am telling you a lie or if I'm not preaching the truth, you don't have to listen to it. But if I am telling you the truth and you don't line up with it, you ought to do something about it.

THE DOCTRINE OF BALAAM

Compromise in the heart of a Christian starts out small. One little indiscretion here, one tiny infidelity there. When he finally realizes he's in deep sin, the snare has him tight.

"I have a few things against you, because you have there those who hold the doctrine of Balaam, who taught Balak to put a stumbling block before the children of Israel, to eat things sacrificed to idols, and to commit sexual immorality. Thus you also have those who hold the doctrine of the Nicolaitans, which thing I hate." (Revelation 2:14–16)

Do you remember the story of Balaam from the Old Testament? We don't have time to go into it here, but you can see the bottom line from the passage above: Balaam led God's people into compromise, immorality, and destruction.

What is the doctrine of Balaam? It's you as a believer influencing another believer to join you in doing something wrong. If you're going to sin, be man or woman enough to sin by yourself. Some people want to justify themselves or feel good about their sins by getting others to do it with them. Sometimes they even throw out this lame lie that now they've found someone who can "understand their struggle."

It's one thing to dive into sin for yourself. That's bad enough. But it's something else when you take someone with you. The sequence in Romans 1 tells us that encouraging others to sin with you is about as low as you can go. (Romans 1:32)

We see it in our church today. We can see it in the church of Pergamum. "Thus you also have those who hold the doctrine of the Nicolaitans, which thing I hate" (Revelation 2:15).

I talked about these cats when we were looking at the church of Ephesus. Jesus commended the Christians in Ephesus for hating the sins of the Nicolaitans. But because of compromise, the church in

Pergamum had accepted the doctrine of the Nicolaitans, which was sexual immorality. That's the other part of the doctrine of Balaam: *accepting* the sin of others.

Do you know of Christians in your circle of influence that are living in sexual sin? Shameful, isn't it? Well, I'll remind you of something that's almost as shameful: Christians who *tolerate* it. Have you said anything (gently) to the person involved? Or do you just gossip about it? Worse, do you let your mind play with the prospect of doing something similar yourself? Tolerating sexual sin in the church has got Balaam written all over it.

WHAT'S YOUR D.O.B.?

That's not "date of birth"; that's "doctrine of Balaam."

What's yours?

What sin do you try to lasso other people into with you? Is there a questionable activity where you find yourself saying to others, "Come on, we're all Christians here; loosen up a little."

Do you love to bad-mouth the company you work for? Do you go to other people and get them to talk about it, too? Doesn't it make you feel just a little bit better to have someone else sinning with you? Doesn't it make you feel less guilty, like you're sharing the burden of guilt?

I know Christian guys who want to watch certain R-rated movies (or worse) but won't, because they feel guilty doing it alone. However, if they can get some buddies from the Bible study to go with them, it's not so bad. "Hey, maybe we can witness to someone at the theater." Yeah, right. Lay it on thick, Jack.

Maybe you don't try to get others to sin with you. Maybe that's not your doctrine of Balaam. Maybe yours is just that you tolerate the sin of others. You look the other way and pretend it isn't there. Now, I'm not saying you have to appoint yourself the Sheriff of Righteousness and go on a crusade to stamp out sin wherever you find it. I'm just saying that if you know Christians that are living in sin and you don't say anything about it, you've just wrapped your arms around the doctrine of Balaam.

"Thus you also have those who hold the doctrine of the Nicolaitans, which thing I hate. Repent, or else I will come to you quickly and will fight against them with the sword of My mouth." (Revelation 2:15–16)

Christians that drag other Christians into sin, or that stand by while Christians sin, will be caught up with the wicked in God's punishment. Repent, or He who holds the double-edged sword will come upon you quickly. In the Old Testament story, Balaam's donkey stopped when she saw the angel of the Lord standing in the middle of the path with His sword unsheathed. Well, you've got more than a donkey warning you to shape up; you've got Jesus Himself. So what's it gonna be?

What's your D.O.B.?

GOD'S PEOPLE HELPING GOD'S ENEMY

Would you believe me if I told you that God's people help God's enemy? It grieves my spirit to see all the church people who help Satan keep Christians marginalized and sidelined. How do they do it? By holding to a doctrine of Balaam.

You're either serving God or you're serving Satan. I don't care how you look at it; I don't care if you want to believe it: You're either helping God and His plan, or you're helping Satan destroy God's plan in somebody else's eyes.

Are you involved in some sin? Have you gotten others involved with you in that sin? If so, I want to give you a warning. God says you are extremely selfish to put someone in with your sin. See, He's not only going to deal with you, but He's going to go get whomever you're sinning with. Someone else is going to come under the judgment of God because of you. Doesn't that just give you the warm fuzzies to know that? Am I helping you today?

God says, "If you're going to sin and you are a believer and you don't repent, I will come on you and I'll do it quickly. You think you're okay and you think you're getting away with it, but I'll come on you quickly. And then I'm going to go after your partners in sin."

If this is you, my friend, you'd better get on your knees quick. Because you do *not* want to be on God's to-do list when He brings punishment. God willing you've got time enough to do the one thing that will set things right: "Repent, or else I will come to you quickly and will fight against them with the sword of My mouth" (Revelation 2:16).

TALK ABOUT SHARP TONGUES

Jesus said that if the believers in Pergamum didn't repent of their compromise, He was going to visit them when He came with the sharp sword of His judgment on the sinners. Let's talk about this swordsman a little.

Have you ever spelled out the word *sword*? (In my neighborhood in Alabama they were call "suh-wards" because you're supposed to pronounce every word the way it is in phonics! Or is that ebonics?) If you take *sword* and drop the *s*, what do you have? The Word. You take the *Word* and add *s* for Son and you've got *sword*.

The Bible says the Word of God is living and active and sharper than—what? A two-edged sword. Jesus Christ is the living Word. The Bible I hold in my hands is alive. That's a fact. I'm going to tell you something I believe: The greatest incarnation of all time was not that Jesus Christ came into the world in the flesh, but that Jesus came alive and put Himself on a page!

And I have it. I have Him! Right in my hands. That's why you can read a regular book over and over and finally drain it; you reach a point where you can't get anything else out of that book. But you can pick up the Bible and read it and it will say something to you today, and you can read it tomorrow and it will say something else to you. You can read it every minute of the day for the rest of your life, and it will *never* be drained. It will say new things to you until the day you check out of your body. Why? Because it's not just a book; it's alive! Hallelujah, what a Savior!

In the beginning was the Word. Everything else is built from there. Without the Word, nothing was made that has been made. Jesus Christ, the mighty Son of God, created all things and holds all things together (Colossians 1:15–17).

Wait till you hear this, because it just blows my little human brain. If Jesus created all things and holds all things together, that means He created *His own mother.* And get this: While He was in her womb He was holding her together. His own mother. Not to mention *the whole universe*. That's beyond me, Jack.

And if He can hold His mother together as an embryo fertilized by the Holy Spirit and keep all creation together, tell me a problem you have that He is left gasping with surprise about. Tell me what problem you have that makes Him say, "Oh, he has *that* problem? Oh no, he's on his own! I can't help him there!" No, no, no, no.

The sword of the Word is living and active, the Bible says. And it's sharp. Take a look:

> For the word of God is living and powerful, and sharper than any two-edged sword, piercing even to the division of soul and spirit, and of joints and marrow, and is a discerner of the thoughts and intents of the heart. (Hebrews 4:12)

Jesus Christ is the Word. He's sharper than a two-edged sword. He can penetrate any situation you have, separate marrow from the bone. He is the penetrating power of all the New Testament church.

Most people think that the "two-edged" reference means slicing and dicing. No, that is incorrect theology. A sword that is double-edged is the sword that *pierces*. It cuts straight down through the bone, even separating bone from marrow. Have you ever donated bone marrow to someone with cancer? It's one of the most painful things you'll ever do because there's no way to deaden the inside of a bone. It is a sacrifice beyond comprehension for someone to do that for another person.

But God says that giving bone marrow is as gentle as a Disney movie compared to what it will be like when He comes with His sword to cut to the core.

Most Christians don't believe that. That's why they give up when they've been praying for someone for a while and haven't seen any change. They think, *Well, that person will just never change.*

What? Change is impossible in that person's life? No sir. Get your ugly, unbelieving self out of the way! My God is the Word with the sword. He penetrates to the marrow of the bone. Don't give up asking for the sword of God's Word to come into anyone's life.

The same is true for you. There is no situation you are in that the Word of God—Jesus Christ—can't penetrate, rightly divide, break down into small bits, and overcome. None. Amen? (Say it out *loud.* I can't hear you!)

On the other hand, there is no sin, no affair, no crime, no compromise, that God's sword cannot penetrate, overcome, or chop into bits, either. When God comes with His sword unsheathed to judge the wicked with the two-edged Word of His mouth, you do not want to be on the pointy end.

A FORGOTTEN DOCTRINE

A long time ago there was this famous preacher named Jonathan Edwards. This cat preached a sermon at the height of the Great Awakening. That sermon was called "Sinners in the Hands of an Angry God." It is a terrible thing, he said, to fall into the hands of an angry God.

Well, my friend, I'm here to tell you it's a *nasty* thing to fall into the hands of an angry God. Nasty, terrible, frightening, you-don't-want-to-go-there, don't-even-ask, *awful* to fall into the hands of an angry God when He comes in judgment.

If you are sinning but don't want to fall into angry hands, you've got one choice: "Repent, or else I will come to you quickly and will fight against them with the sword of My mouth" (Revelation 2:16).

Repentance. It's a lost art in the church today. I think there are a lot of people that believe they are Christians but really are not. Why? Because they haven't repented. They've said words, but I don't think they've repented. No repentance, no salvation. Then there are all those Christians living inconsistent lives in Christ due to their lack of repentance. Without repentance you cannot be right with God. Don't skim over that statement! Without repentance you *cannot* be right with God.

Our repentance is so often shallow. We're not grieved that we've sinned against almighty God; we're just sorry we got caught. The words we sometimes throw up at Him aren't true repentance; they're things we hope will keep us from getting disciplined. Just like bratty kids. I'll tell you what, though: God knows the difference.

What is God's definition of *repentance?* If it's the thing that gets us on the friendly side of the sword of God's Word, it's important that we get it right.

The Greek word behind *repentance* is *metanoia.* It means to change your mind. It's godly sorrow over sin. It's turning away from wickedness and dead works and turning toward God and His glory. Metanoia means you make yourself of a different mind—you force your mind to change so that it lines up with the Word of God. That's true repentance, and it's a lost doctrine in our church today.

Here's a picture of metanoia. Let's say you're walking east. Now you turn 180 degrees and start walking west. You were headed toward Miami, and now your nose is pointed toward L.A. That's metanoia. It means you turn completely around from going the way of sin, and you start going God's way.

I don't know about you, but most of the time I don't do 180-degree repentance. No. Most of the time I do 360-degree repentance. That's when I stop, say, "Thank You, Lord, for forgiving me, amen," and then *boom!* I'm back going in the same direction as before. Get myself dizzy.

Am I the only one? How many times have you confessed something in your life and find yourself still doing it today? You haven't metanoia-ed. In order to truly repent you've got to have a complete change of heart about the sin you're in. That is true repentance: You've got to change your mind about God 100 percent, you've got to change your mind about the sin, and you've got to change your mind about yourself. Do you understand that? God does not accept our little mediocre confessions. He only accepts true repentance. Without repentance, you cannot be right with God.

But guess who doesn't want you to repent? Guess who likes it when you live in sin and wrap your arms around compromise? You guessed it. Satan can't stand true repentance. He flees from the pure in heart. He does all he can to prevent metanoia from happening. He's taught the whole world to think it's weak to admit when you're wrong. If you admit you're wrong, you're admitting you're imperfect and other people will get one up on you.

"Don't repent," he says. "Don't do it. You don't have to. Try this instead: Blame someone else."

Do you realize that the world is being taught today, especially through psychology, that you are not the problem? It's everybody else's fault. If you really want to know, it was your mom's fault for the way she held you when you were two days old! And it's definitely your grandmother's fault on the other side because if your grandmother would have held your mother right, your mother would have held you right!

This marriage falling apart is not your fault; it's your spouse's fault. Because if your spouse were more like you, everything would be just fine. The only difference is that if your spouse were just like you, he or she never would have married you!

Your kids are rebelling? Not your fault. It's society's fault for being so violent. It's hormones or syndromes or MTV or attention deficit disorder. It's anything but your fault. Why? Because, poor soul, you are a v-i-c-t-i-m.

Well, I'll tell you straight out: If you've got the idea that everything that's happening to you is somebody else's fault, *it's impossible for you to repent*. That means it's impossible for you to be right with God. And you'll be on the pointy end when He comes.

Surrender the fight. Go ahead and admit your sin. God won't be mad at you if you admit your sin. That's what we tend to imagine, isn't it? We think that if we can just keep from having to admit that we're to blame, then somehow we really *aren't* to blame, at least not officially. But God sees into the heart, into the division of bone and marrow, amen? We think He's mad at us *if* we confess our sin. But the truth is He's mad at us *until* we admit our sin.

GET METANOIA-ED—IT PAYS

"Repent, or else I will come to you quickly and will fight against them with the sword of My mouth." (Revelation 2:16)

Do you see the two groups in this passage?

He says to repent or He will come to *you* quickly and will fight against *them* with His double-edged Word. *You* refers to the Christians that have allowed compromise in their own lives or have tolerated sin in the lives of other Christians. *Them* are the Nicolaitans—those that try to sweep sexual promiscuity under the blanket of Christianity—and the pagans who worship where Satan's throne is.

Jesus Christ cares about pagans and sinners as well as Christians. But in this letter, His eye is on the Christians. His warning is to those believers that have shown their love for Him by standing firm in the face of persecution, but that have gone lax and now tolerate sexual sin.

His anger will come against sinners. But Christians who shrink back from persecution and embrace sin will be included in His punishment. Not to the point that they lose their salvation but to the point that they will wish they'd never flirted with the doctrine of Balaam.

This earth belongs to the enemy of God. He is the prince of this world. That's why it's not pleasant living here and being a child of God. We live our whole lives behind enemy lines! The price of fidelity to God is often persecution. In the face of persecution for their faith, many Christians turn to compromise. They stand firm on some issues but faint away from others. Nevertheless, God expects His children to stand for Him. If they maintain their position of compromise, they will suffer alongside the wicked when Jesus brings the double-edged sword of His punishment. Their only hope—and ours—is to repent.

REPENT WITH YOUR FEET!

A certain man had two sons. Don't you love stories that start out like that? Here it is from Jesus' mouth:

> "A man had two sons, and he came to the first and said, 'Son, go, work today in my vineyard.' He answered and said, 'I will not,' but afterward he regretted it and went. Then he came to the second and said likewise. And he answered and said, 'I go, sir,' but he did not go. Which of the two did the will of his father?" (Matthew 21:28–31a)

There is no such thing as repentance without new actions. You cannot say, "God, forgive me for what I've done," and then continue down a mediocre road. The first son said "no," but then changed his mind. He quit disobeying and got his life lined up with the will of his father. He metanoia-ed.

But his words weren't enough.

Even his change of mind was not enough.

He had to add *actions* to his words. Not only did he line up with what his father wanted, be he also *accomplished* what his father wanted. That is true repentance in the believer's life. There is no repentance without new actions. If you've said the words but your actions are the same as before, you haven't repented.

God will give you the power to walk in His ways—to abandon that old sin and have a pure heart before Him—but He's waiting for you to be willing to leave it behind. He's waiting for you to change your mind about the sin, about yourself, and about Him.

Return to the faith you had at the beginning.

Stand up for what you know is right, even if the world takes you to the wall for it. Better to be righteous and dead in Christ than alive and in sin when Jesus Christ comes.

CHAPTER FIVE

Thyatira:
ONE MINUTE
TILL MIDNIGHT

What do you tolerate?

If you're like me, you tolerate loud noises if there's good reason. If someone's building on to your house for you, you put up with a little pounding and sawing. If your dogs are going nuts barking at Mormons coming to your door, you put up with that.

You tolerate obnoxious people if they're family (and if they go home after the holiday is over).

You tolerate paying too much for things if you're in a hurry.

You tolerate pain if it means you're going to feel better afterward.

You even tolerate a messy house or office or car or desk if other matters are more pressing. (Other matters are always more pressing for me!)

Tolerance is the battle cry of the New Age. Don't be narrow-minded, Jack. Be open-minded. Accept everyone. It doesn't matter what you believe as long as you're *sincere*, right?

It cracks me up that New Agers are tolerant of everyone but conservative Christians. Every religion is okay with them so long as no one stands up and says one way is right and all other ways are wrong. These heroes of tolerance can get downright intolerant.

In fact we live in a culture that is intolerant of intolerance.

You can't stand up anymore and say someone's living wrong. Well, you can, but get ready to meet the press, baby. "You're so narrow-minded. You're so hateful. You're so insensitive to other people's beliefs. How are they hurting you?" They're not hurting me; they're hurting themselves. I'm just trying to help them get back on the path.

"Who are you to stand in judgment over anyone else?" I'm a servant of the living God, that's who. I'm a high priest of God Almighty, a child of light, holding out the Word of life to a crooked and perverse generation. Ooh, I make a lot of people mad.

Our society demands in-your-face tolerance. "I *dare* you to not tolerate me. You reject me and I'll slap a lawsuit on you faster than you can say dial-a-lawyer."

Isn't it amazing that today if you want to discipline someone—in your church, in your business, in your family—it is interpreted as insensitivity and a lack of love? Suddenly the problem isn't them; it's you. You're sexist, you're racist, you're homophobic, you're narrow, you're insensitive. Today's definition of love insists that you remain "totally accepting," that you never say anything negative or critical (unless you're talking about evangelical believers). You're not allowed to call for change.

Parents, too, have swallowed a bunch of psychobabble about discipline. Now the going idea is that if you really love your kids, you won't discipline them. Oh, my goodness! Be their buddy. Empower them. Let their inner child have authority in your household.

There are some Christian parents out there who buy into this. And they've got some bad kids, Jack. *Whoo.* Wild. Disobedient. Their parents won't discipline them—but boy, they'll love them. "Jimmy's just going through a stage right now. If we love him and accept him, we know he'll stop shooting people from his window." Relatives don't want to keep these kids. They're so bad my dogs don't even want to play with 'em. They go hide in the woods until the kids leave. And I've got some bad dogs!

The world thinks happiness is the absence of all restrictions—"If you loved me you wouldn't put these restrictions on me." But I'm telling you that the Bible says casting off all restraint is not the path to pleasing God. No. Accepting someone without calling for change isn't biblical love at all; it's selfish love.

This was the problem at the First Community Church of Thyatira. They tolerated something (someone, actually) that should have been thrown out instead. Back at Ephesus the believers held tight to doctrinal purity—but had lost their love. The believers at Thyatira loved, but tossed doctrinal purity out the window. The truth is, you've got to have both in balance to walk the Christian walk.

LADY LYDIA'S LEGACY

Thyatira was probably the smallest city of the seven mentioned in Revelation 2 and 3. Because of this, the town was not too heavily influenced by Rome, which is another way of saying the Emperor pretty much didn't care about Thyatira. That's why archeological ruins in the city don't have any of the Roman temples or altars to Roman emperors. Thyatira was influential, though, for two reasons: One, it was on the major trade road between Pergamum and Sardis; two, it made purple dye.

Remember Lydia from Acts? She was the seller of purple whom Paul met in Philippi. Acts 16 tells us Lydia was from Thyatira. Turns out Thyatira was known for its exotic dyes and cloths. Purple dye was rare and difficult to make, so it was very expensive. Only kings and nobility wore garments that had been soaked in it. Thyatira had the goods, which made it a draw for the rich and famous of Asia Minor.

Just because Thyatira was the smallest city of the seven—and may also have been the smallest church of the seven—doesn't mean it was insignificant. Did you know this is Jesus' longest letter of the seven? He devotes twelve whole verses to this church in Thyatira. Smyrna only got four. The closest any other church's letter got to this was the one to Laodicea, which was nine verses. The others range from six to seven verses. Thyatira may have felt insignificant as a city or church, but it was superimportant to almighty God.

That's God's way, isn't it? Seeing significance where man sees insignificance. Counting as nothing what man values above all else.

Let's talk about Lydia for a minute. I believe she came back to her hometown and started a Christian church there. She was probably a wealthy lady because of her trade and used her means and influence—along with a big helping of courageous faith—to start a church in a little town. To this day that church lives on in the pages of Scripture.

What God can do with one person who makes himself fully available to Him is unbelievable. I don't care who you are, what you think of yourself, how small you think you are, or how little talent you think you have, God can do miraculous things with you. Will you let Him?

"For the eyes of the LORD move to and fro throughout the earth that He may strongly support those whose heart is completely His." (2 Chronicles 16:9a, NASB)

The book you hold in your hands is the product of an illegitimate child. That's right. I was born eight days after my mother turned fifteen, an unwanted child born to an unmarried teenage girl during a depression. We were so poor that if you walked to the backyard and threw the dog a bone, he had to call a fair catch to keep the neighbors from running over and trying to get it.

Nobody expects very much of a kid like that. But look what God has done. He has taken an illegitimate child, turned him around, saved him, and given him a legitimate ministry.

That's what God can do for every one of us when we turn ourselves over to Him. Lydia was just one woman, but she may have founded a church written into the final book of Holy Scripture. And think of it— the Word of God will stand forever! What an awesome tribute to this woman's step of faith and obedience.

Lydia's legacy was a church that was well spoken of by Jesus Christ and that made it into the Bible. Hutch's legacy will be his family, his ministry, and Antioch Bible Church. What will your legacy be?

IT'S A SETUP

When Jesus dictates His letter to the church at Thyatira, He follows His usual pattern: First He says what they've been doing well, then He lets 'em have it with a warning—followed up with a quick shot of hope. He starts with the good:

> "And to the angel of the church in Thyatira write,
>
> 'These things says the Son of God, who has eyes like a flame of fire, and His feet like fine brass: "I know your works, love, service, faith, and your patience; and as for your works, the last are more than the first."'" (Revelation 2:18–19)

I wonder if by now John was starting to shake his head. "Oh, no, here it comes. He's buttering them up."

This church was doing all right, it seems to me. God knew them as a loving church, a serving church, a faithful church, and a patient church. Does God know your church that way? Does He think of you as an individual in that way?

Good works

Jesus knew them for their good works, too. Not only were they doing good works, but they were also increasing in them. They were making strides on the right path and their new programs were pleasing to God. Now, I've launched a few church programs in my day, and I can tell you that I didn't feel God's blessing on all of them. How great would it be to have Jesus Himself come down with words like these? "Those new works you're doing? Thumbs up, baby, you're right on track."

Love

Jesus said, "I know your love." Thyatira was a church that loved like crazy. No one could accuse them of leaving their first love. We'll find out later that their love was out of balance. It was all acceptance and no spine. But for now it's enough to know that they were loving folks. If you showed up at one of their church potlucks with nothing but a fork and an appetite, you'd never go away hungry.

Service

"I know your service." This was a serving church. Wouldn't it be great to be known as a serving church? A *working* church? A roll-up-your-sleeves-and-get-it-done church? Next time you're at your fellowship on a Sunday morning, look around. Look at all the sound and lighting equipment and musical instruments. What set-up work has been done before you cruised in through the front door five minutes before the service? I'll bet you didn't know that all those things just march in there by themselves, did you? They drive themselves over, get out, come in, and just line up like that. Amazing, isn't it? Late Saturday night the chairs unfold themselves, file in there, and spread themselves out. The lights know exactly where to be to light the pastor.

I don't think so.

The only way the local church exists is because of service. No service, no church. As a pastor, I'm not into overworking church members and burning them out, but I am into motivating people to get up and serve so the church can do its job and they can become part of something. If you're feeling lonely in your church, like nobody knows you and no one would care if you stopped coming, *then get busy serving.* Don't just come and sit; serve somewhere. Put your oar in the water, and pull with all the strength God gives you! That's the nature of church.

Fearless, faithful, and patient

Thyatira was also a faithful church. That sounds good, doesn't it? "Our church is faithful." As we learned at Smyrna, you can't have faith and fear at the same time. So we could say that Thyatira was a fearless church, too. Fearless and faithful.

Thyatira was also patient. The risen Lord Jesus said so Himself: "I know your patience." Can you imagine Him saying those same words to you? Ooh, that gets just a little bit convicting! Is your church known as a patient church? Are you known as a patient believer?

Have you ever made the mistake (I mean, "had the privilege") of praying for more patience? Don't do it! However, if you find yourself thinking that God does not hear your prayers and you want to conduct an experiment, go ahead and pray for patience. Just don't say I didn't warn you.

Once a lady came to my office and asked me, "Pastor, would you pray that I would have more patience with my family?"

"Sure," I said. "You want me to pray right now?"

"Oh, yes, pastor. Thank you!"

"Okay, let's pray."

"Lord, I just want to thank You that every one of this dear sister's kids are about to start going absolutely nuts. Thank You, Father, that her husband will stop listening to her. Thank You that her car is about to lose its transmission and that the hard drive on her computer will fry like an egg. We praise You for all the problems and tribulations You're about to send—"

"Wait a minute!" she cried. "What in the world are you praying for?"

"You wanted me to pray for your patience, didn't you?"

"Yes, but I didn't mean—"

"Sister, this is step number one. The Bible says you obtain patience through trouble, trials, and tribulation. I was just trying to help you out!" She didn't like me very much after that.

The kind of patience Jesus was commending the Christians in Thyatira for was the kind that only comes through trials. It is the ability to suffer for a long time without changing your countenance. It's the kind of patience that puts hopeless marriages back together, reconciles divided churches, gets employees and employers talking to one another, and draws us back into fellowship with God. This is the kind of patience He has with us. Praise God for that! Otherwise He would have punted you and me a long time ago.

LOVE THAT WASN'T

This church was doing pretty well, wouldn't you say? They had some great qualifications. If you've been with me this long, though, you know something's coming. You can feel them being set up for something, can't you? The Thyatiran Christians are all in a good mood over how great Jesus thinks they're doing. They're feeling generous. Now would be a good time to hit these folks up for a loan!

But Jesus asks them for more than that.

He asks them to change.

"I know your works, love, service, faith, and your patience; and as for your works, the last are more than the first. Nevertheless I have a few things against you, because you allow that woman Jezebel, who calls herself a prophetess, to teach and beguile My servants to commit sexual immorality and to eat things sacrificed to idols." (Revelation 2:19–20)

The problem with this loving church was that it practiced an imbalanced kind of love. It was the kind of "love" that accepted the sinner *and* the sin—and never once called for change. It was the kind of love that threw open its doors to the world and told folks they were okay just the way they were. It was the kind of love that allowed false teachers to come in and lead good Christians into sin and idolatry.

It was a too-tolerant kind of love.

The kind of love the church at Thyatira had begun practicing was based on the world's love, which says, "I'm going to accept you the way you are, and I'm going to prove how much I love you by letting you stay the way you are."

They must have had a lot of love, too, or Jesus wouldn't have praised them for it. But He also sternly warned them, "You're walking on the knife edge of a great chasm. You're moving away from true biblical love, and you're about to fall into what the world calls love." Worldly love says, "I want to do whatever it takes to make you comfortable." God's love says, "I'm going to do everything it takes to make you like Christ."

God calls us to accept the sinner, not the sin. Yes, anyone can come into our church. The doors of Antioch Bible Church are open to all. But if you're going to keep coming back and if you want to enter into fellowship with the believers in our church, the pastor's going to have a little talk with you about your lifestyle. See, God loves us too much to leave us as we are. We'll never be Christlike if we're just left to our own efforts.

Picture a really tolerant NFL coach. He doesn't ask his players to work out or show up for practices. He doesn't get on 'em for penalties or fumbles or missed tackles. He just accepts them and loves on them and hopes they'll somehow float up into excellence on the ball field. Doesn't work. The best coaches I ever had expected me to shoot for the high mark they set for me. If they challenged me to change, if they got in my face just a little bit, I didn't think they were unloving or intolerant; I thought they wanted the best for me and the team.

What did Jesus have against the church at Thyatira? He said they'd gone overboard on love and acceptance to the point that now a false teacher had come in and was leading the faithful astray.

They say nature hates a vacuum. (I must be a natural guy, then, because I hate vacuuming, too!) Air tries to rush into a vacuum to fill it and equalize the pressure around it. I'm here to tell you that Satan *loves* a vacuum—a vacuum of truth, that is. Whenever truth grows weak, he's got his shoulder against the door, trying to muscle his way in. He jumps on the throne if Jesus hasn't been set there. He sets up shop real quick. Before you know it, he's pumping out sin like nobody's business. That's why new believers are in such danger from the cults. These excited new converts want to follow Jesus, but there's a truth vacuum; they don't know the Word; they don't know who they are or what they have in Christ. That's when the satanic counterfeiters rush in with distorted, warped information and try to pick these young believers off.

In Thyatira's case, a certain woman had infiltrated the church and was bringing believers down big time.

THAT...THAT...JEZEBEL!

I don't think the woman's name was really Jezebel. Could have been, I guess, but I don't think so. Jesus talked about the Nicolaitans as those teaching the doctrine of Balaam. Later in Revelation He talks about Babylon, which most Bible scholars believe was a reference to Rome. Revelation is apocalyptic literature, which means among other things that it uses lots of symbolism. So I don't think you would have found the name "Jezebel" in Thyatira's church directory.

In a way, it's better for us that she isn't named. If she were, this might be a little side-note Scripture, just a bit of history. (As with Anna, the prophetess at the Temple.) But by giving this false teacher a code name, Jesus urges us to look for the *spirit* of Jezebel wherever we are, wherever we live. That's application.

I think this woman was a deacon's wife or elder's wife. That's my own opinion. Maybe she was even the pastor's wife—the wife of the angel of Thyatira. She had to be someone very prominent to have so much influence with the church members. Whoever she was, Jesus carefully chose a name to describe what she was like.

To find out what He meant, let's take a short walk on the Old Testament side.

JEZEBEL: THE ORIGINAL ARTICLE

What kind of woman was the original Jezebel? She must've been pretty bad news because I don't hear many people naming their daughters

Jezebel. I don't even name any of my *dogs* Jezebel. It's not the sort of name you like to toss around.

> And it came to pass, as though it had been a trivial thing for him to walk in the sins of Jeroboam the son of Nebat, that [King Ahab] took as wife Jezebel the daughter of Ethbaal, king of the Sidonians; and he went and served Baal and worshiped him. (1 Kings 16:31)

Catch that? Ahab the king of Israel married Jezebel and *boom!* he's a Baal worshiper. Just like that. I doubt that he and his wife ever sat down to discuss what church they were going to, or whether they should sign their kids up for AWANA. When Ahab said "I do" to Jezebel, he married the whole nasty package—including her despicable religion.

You can readily believe there wasn't anything much in Ahab's heart before the wedding. He must've been looking for something to worship. Then along comes this hot princess with this exotic religion, one that allowed him all kinds of sexual freedoms. And *bang!* He's there, baby. Satan loves a vacuum.

With the king and the queen both promoting Baal worship, you get a good picture of how popular the prophets of the true God were. When this chick got the power, watch out!

> For so it was, while Jezebel massacred the prophets of the LORD, that Obadiah had taken one hundred prophets and hidden them, fifty to a cave, and had fed them with bread and water. (1 Kings 18:4)

It doesn't say she had the prophets of the true God massacred; it says *she* massacred them. I wouldn't put it past her. Not by a long shot. I can see her going from throat to throat with an old rusty knife, cutting down the prophets of God. I can see her *liking* it. This woman was unbelievable.

Not content to drive her husband and family down the highway to hell, Jezebel pulled a whole nation along behind her—a nation that would suffer destruction just as she was ultimately destroyed.

Now Jesus comes to this small church at Thyatira and says *they* have a Jezebel of their own. They've opened the doors to this woman, and she's leading the people into sin and idolatry. She's on the same express lane to hell as her predecessor—and pickin' up speed.

Chances are she was so intimidating that nobody dared stand up to her. Back in the Old Testament, God raised up that salty old prophet Elijah to go toe-to-toe with the original Jezzy. Here in the book of Revelation, Jesus Christ takes on the job Himself.

THE SPIRIT OF JEZEBEL

For a long time I couldn't figure out why Jesus Christ, the head of the church, would relate the Old Testament Jezebel to anything or anyone in a New Testament church. I really struggled with what characteristics of Jezebel might've been coming through in the church at Thyatira— and the church today, in believers. But when I discovered what it was, it woke me up to what's happening. If I do my job right, soon you'll see the correlation between this Jezebel and modern believers.

"Nevertheless I have a few things against you, because you allow that woman Jezebel, who calls herself a prophetess, to teach and beguile My servants to commit sexual immorality and to eat things sacrificed to idols. And I gave her time to repent of her sexual immorality, and she did not repent. Indeed I will cast her into a sickbed, and those who commit adultery with her into great tribulation, unless they repent of their deeds. And I will kill her children with death. And all the churches shall know that I am He who searches the minds and hearts. And I will give to each one of you according to your works." (Revelation 2:20–24)

Let's look at the characteristics of a modern-day Jezebel. First, she infiltrates God's people and tries to silence the true Word of God. The Old Testament Jezebel became queen of Israel and tried to cut off the worship of the true and living God. She rounded up all the prophets she could find and eliminated them herself (such a personal touch!). The "Jezebel" at Thyatira tried to silence the truth by setting herself up as a prophet in the church and by teaching false doctrine.

The word *prophecy* has a changed meaning in how we use it today. Today, prophecy is not hearing new words from God; it's telling truth that's already been written in the Bible. I am a modern-day prophet: I teach what has been written already in God's Word. A modern-day Jezebel, then, is someone who will try to influence a truth teller in such a way that his life and witness are destroyed, thus silencing the Word of God.

Second, a modern-day Jezebel doesn't have to be a woman. The spirit of Jezebel is alive and well in the hearts of men as well as women. Just as the doctrine of Balaam could come from a woman, so the spirit of Jezebel could be seen in a man.

Third—and here's the heart of it—someone operating in the spirit of Jezebel tries to use God and His people for his or her own purposes. The spirit of Jezebel can be seen in false teachers who infiltrate the church to gather a following, get rich, and serve their own lusts. They usually do this by saying they've received "new truth" from God.

New truth—ha! If anyone who tells you God has given him something new, just politely look him in the eye and call him a liar. The sixty-six books God has given us are complete for what we need in the present day. Why should God decide to give me something new when I haven't learned to live what's in the sixty-six He's already given? There's no need for new material. Ken Hutcherson has all he can handle between the covers of his Bible...and so do you.

I'll tell you something else that reflects the spirit of Jezebel in our churches today. In a big church like mine, there are lots of good-looking single ladies. Men with the spirit of Jezebel will try to use the church and God's people as a means to getting what they want. They'll come to church just to meet women. They know some Christian women are desperate to get married and might be willing to "put out" before marriage if they dangle the M-word in front of them. They'll do everything they can just to get next to you and pretend that they're spiritual, and they will ruin your life by having sex with you and then dropping you like a short putt. Parasites and predators. Male Jezebels, every one.

I know single women who are the same way. They come to church not to learn about God, but to find out who's there and who could take care of them. That's coming to God and His people as an excuse to get what you want when you want it. If this is you, I'm giving you a warning from God: Don't use His people to try to get your way, because you won't like what He does to Jezebels.

I want to talk about one more shape a Jezebel might take in a church today: lost pastors. Remember, Jezebels are those who want to use God and His church to get what they want. I know pastors who head up churches when they don't even believe in God. Why are they in the pulpit preaching sermons? Because they think it's a cushy job and an easy paycheck. I'm telling you, the Rapture is going to come, and the following Sunday there are still going to be plenty of pulpits with pastors in them. Hirelings and Jezebels. (That's why it's up to you to be discerning about whom you let lead you spiritually.)

Jezebels, then, are men or women who infiltrate the church, try to silence God's Word, and use God and His people as means to their own selfish ends. Know anybody like that?

I NEED MY SPACE

God doesn't think too highly of Jezebels. Huh-uh. He will bring judgment upon them and all who get caught up into the sins of the spirit of Jezebel. What I'm surprised by is that God actually gives these false-teaching, truth-silencing, lust-chasing people time to change their ways.

> "I gave her time to repent of her sexual immorality, and she did not repent. Indeed I will cast her into a sickbed, and those who commit adultery with her into great tribulation, unless they repent of their deeds. And I will kill her children with death.

And all the churches shall know that I am He who searches the minds and hearts. And I will give to each one of you according to your works. But to you I say, and to the rest in Thyatira, as many as do not have this doctrine, and who have not known the depths of Satan, as they call them, I will put on you no other burden. But hold fast what you have till I come." (Revelation 2:21–25)

What does it mean by saying that Jesus gave Jezebel time to repent? Some versions say He gave her *space* to repent. What does that mean? When we say we're going to give someone some space, we mean we're going to back off for a while. We mean we're going to take the pressure off and give the person some time or room or freedom.

Is that what Jesus is saying to Thyatira about Jezebel, that He's backing off to let her find herself? Is He saying, "I'm going to give this poor dear some space; I'm not going to let my Holy Spirit convict her of wrong"? No, no, no, no.

I think it means He gave her opportunity to change her ways, perhaps to turn to God. "I gave her the chance to repent. I gave her time to turn around," He says. "I had my servants there telling her truth. I was available if she would come. But she wouldn't."

God holds the door open for all who will to come to Him. That's the patience of God Paul talks about in Romans 2:4 and 9:22. The reason we're still here right now is because Jesus Christ is still holding the door for anyone to come in. But I'm here to tell you that the door will not stay open forever. There will come a time when the door is shut, and after that, too bad.

One day God got Noah and all the animals into the ark, and He shut that door. They could probably hear their friends and neighbors outside, beating on the ark, shouting for Noah to open up and let them in.

But they couldn't, even if they'd wanted to.

Why? Because *God* had shut the door. He is the One "who opens and no one shuts, and shuts and no one opens" (Revelation 3:7).

God is giving the world time to repent, too. Time to see the light and get on in. That's what Jesus is talking about with Jezebel. He gave her plenty of opportunity to turn. But when she persisted in her sinful ways, He let the door swing shut. Check it out: Jesus doesn't call Jezebel to repentance in this passage. He calls the people who sin with her to repent, but He doesn't offer Jezebel the same opportunity. Her chance is over.

Don't miss this. Sometimes God waits until someone's last breath to say the door is shut for him to repent. Other times He shuts the door before the person dies. It's like Pharaoh hardening his heart: After repeated refusals of the gift of life and the way of truth, God will grant a person's request and give him over to his lust. I'm not saying repentance is impossible for people like that, just that it's extremely unlikely.

FRUITS WORTHY OF REPENTANCE

When Jesus says He gives time to repent, I believe He's saying that He's giving people time to *bear out* their repentance. He's talking about an amount of time to prove that they have changed.

In the previous chapter I talked about repentance in regard to Pergamum. That was the *act* of repentance—slammin' on the brakes and turning 180 degrees, changing your mind to line up with God's Word. I think we see in Thyatira the *essence* of repentance—proving that a change has happened by (in the words of my boy John the Baptist) producing fruits worthy of repentance. Jesus says, "I'm going to give you space and time to grow in repentance."

Growing in repentance. That's different from just repenting. Don't get me wrong: Nothing good happens without genuine repentance. But it doesn't end there. It is a process of working out that repentance day and night for the long haul. God says, "I do not just hear what you say; I am going to watch you walk. I'm going to walk with you and I'm going to watch you walk with Me." When you have proven your change with weeks and months and years of living anew, God says you have repented.

People come up and say to me, "Pastor, will you forgive me for what I did?" I say, "Of course I will forgive you, but I don't trust you." I want to see them walking a different path for a while. I want to see their lives change. Until then they're forgiven; I'm just not going to make myself vulnerable to them again.

I forgive you, but you aren't going to have access to my family or my finances. You're forgiven, but you aren't going to be on staff for a while, because there are a lot of sheep out there that take their cues from me. If they think that I trust you, they're going to submit themselves to you.

Isn't repentance awesome? This is Thyatira-type repentance. It's the kind of repentance that produces spiritual fruit.

When you become a Christian, the Holy Spirit comes in and starts producing fruit. It may be raisins or it may be some old dried-up prunes, but at least they'll get you on the move! Hear this: *The spiritual fruit in your life is going to be equal to the degree of your repentance.*

Back in my NFL days—before I became a Christian and before I was married—some women would come up and say, "Hey, how you doing, big guy? I'd like to go out with you, and man, we could have a good time." Now, as a nonbeliever did I sit there and think, *Woman, are you trying to tempt me?* No! I'd go, "Um, um, um, I'm *bad.* Look at this. I'm a stud king!" (Don't get too excited: You can find studs on snow tires, too.)

When I became a Christian, though, and would be propositioned, something was different. Watch out, here comes guilt! The conviction of the Holy Spirit would fall on me and I would run away. What was the difference? My true repentance was producing spiritual fruit. If you don't have spiritual fruit, maybe you need to ask yourself (and God) if you've really repented.

"Indeed I will cast [Jezebel] into a sickbed, and those who commit adultery with her into great tribulation, unless they repent of their deeds. And I will kill her children with death. And all the churches shall know that I am He who searches the minds and hearts. And I will give to each one of you according to your works." (Revelation 2:22–23)

Have you fallen in with a Jezebel? Have you gone along with sin even though you know it's wrong? Maybe it's a Christian or even someone sinning right in the church. You've gone along with it. Why? Because it feeds your pet lust or greed.

If so, you'd best back away real quick. Jesus Christ is coming, and He's going to bring judgment—not just on that Jezebel but on all who sin with her. Who are her "children" but those she begets by her false teaching? Her followers. Sure, this person may have led you into sin when you weren't looking and before you knew it there you were. But now that you know, what are you going to do? Great tribulation is coming on you for your participation in this Jezebel's sin.

"But to you I say, and to the rest in Thyatira, as many as do not have this doctrine, and who have not known the depths of Satan, as they call them, I will put on you no other burden. But hold fast what you have till I come." (Revelation 2:24–25)

The depths of Satan?

What in the world is that?

Most likely this woman in Thyatira was teaching the Christians that she possessed mysteries that she could reveal to the initiated. These were the so-called "depths of God." If you've poked around in a Bible dictionary any, you may have come across the term *Gnosticism*. That was a heresy that started in the first or second century A.D. It said that you could get salvation by learning all the deep secrets, the hidden knowledge, of God. These mostly involved sexual deviancy. This is what this Jezebel was probably teaching them. She called them the depths of God. God called them what they were: the depths of Satan. Right out of the pit.

God had given this Jezebel time to repent. If she had only known that it was two minutes before midnight. The clock was ticking, and her time was almost up. By the time Jesus came to dictate this letter to John, her time *was* up. He was only appealing to the Christians to repent. He was holding the door open for them. "Come on home. Repent. Leave her ways. But be quick, because this door won't always be open."

I think He was calling on the church to kick this chick out. He was appealing to the Christians who had sinned with her to repent and to join those who hadn't sinned with her, who had held themselves apart from her false teachings and given the woman the boot. He was calling for all of them to come together and form a Better-than-Elijah committee and in the name of God stand up to this Jezebel.

Is there a Jezebel in your church or circle of influence? Is he or she leading the faithful into sin? If you have ears to hear the One who has eyes like a flame of fire and feet like fine brass, then obey His Word and show that person the door. *Fast.*

Produce fruit in keeping with repentance. Show the reality of your new life by walking out the change day by day. Grow in your repentance and cultivate good fruit. Leave false teaching and deal with false teachers.

Do it all while the door's still open.

THERE'S JUST SOMETHING ABOUT THAT NAME

In the entire book of Revelation, Jesus Christ only refers to Himself as the Son of God in one place—right here: "These things says the Son of God, who has eyes like a flame of fire, and His feet like fine brass" (Revelation 2:18b).

If this is the only time He puts that name on again, don't you think what He's about to say is going to be important? I think He's pleading with the Christians in Thyatira who have gotten caught up in the sin of this Jezebel.

And I think He's pleading with us, too—almost begging us to come out of the sin we've found ourselves enjoying. I think He's feeling the door about to close. I think He's holding the door open for us to repent, but the window of opportunity is shutting. He's given us time and He wants us to come. But if we haven't come in obedience, maybe we'll come if He pleads.

What will it be? Oh, my brother or sister, now is the time for repentance! Today is the day of salvation. The ark is ready, and the rain clouds are overhead. What's that wet on your cheek? The rain is coming. The floods are coming. Disease and tribulation are coming. Back out of that sin! Disentangle yourself. Run back to the Father who is waiting. Repent and stick to your repentance. Get inside where it's safe and dry.

While the door's still open.

CHAPTER SIX

Sardis:

ALMOST (BUT NOT QUITE) TERMINAL

When the church at Sardis collected her mail one fine day in A.D. 95, she must have wished she'd never gone to the mailbox. Have you ever received mail like that? After you opened the letter, you wanted to run after the postman yelling, "Take it back! Take it back!"

Maybe it was a bill that shocked you all the way to your billfold.

Maybe it was a Dear John or Dear Jane letter that said, "Hit the road, Jack."

Maybe it was a note from the doctor with a lab report you didn't want to see.

Maybe it was a rejection notice from some college you'd set your heart on.

Maybe it was your child's report card with grades that were miles below C-level.

The letter to Sardis was postmarked from heaven, from the Son of

God Himself, and delivered by a letter carrier everyone knew and no one felt inclined to argue with: the apostle John. This was no Hallmark card covered with hearts and flowers and fuzzy kittens. In fact, it was more like a letter bomb. The impact shook that church so hard that it never really recovered.

The words of the Lord Jesus to the church at Sardis cut them to the core. It stabbed them so deeply that some couldn't respond or rebound from those stern words.

His basic message? You think you're healthy. You think you're doing just fine. You think you can cruise through on your charm, good looks, and reputation. But you're wrong. In fact, you are so near death that I can barely pick up a heartbeat. If you don't change soon, if you don't repent fast, you'll be toes up, room temperature.

Oooh! How would you like to get a note like that from your doctor? Do you think it might get your attention? Do you think it might make you sit up and take notice?

Jesus said to Sardis, "You've got a name. People say you're alive. But I know better. My eyes are like a flame of fire, and they see right through your masquerade."

WAKE UP!

Sardis was a city that was essentially dead. It had all the trappings of life—population, commerce, worship—but it was on life support. Same with the church's members there: They were spiritually dead, full of apathy and selfishness. I think they had been alive before and were resting on their accomplishments. They felt they had the Christian life down pat, so they didn't bother to keep an eye out for sin. Consequently, sin slipped in when they weren't watching. It would be their downfall.

You see, that kind of double life won't cut it when you belong to Christ. You can't serve God and self at the same time. You might think you can pull it off, you might fool some of the people some of the time or even all the people all the time, but you won't fool the Lord of the church. You can't pull the wool over eyes that are on fire! And I'll tell you flat out: If you ever want to kill your spiritual life, just start making *you* the center of everything.

A few years ago I heard about one of those annoying national surveys where they interview folks about the major problems in America. This particular survey uncovered two problems absolutely central to our country: ignorance and indifference. In a follow-up survey, one of the pollsters walked up to a lady in the mall and said, "We have come to the conclusion that America has two great problems. Which problem do you think is greatest: ignorance or indifference?" The lady didn't want to be bothered, so she said, "I don't *know* and I don't *care!*"

It's one thing for the world to be apathetic about others; it's another thing for a church to be indifferent. Do you know what *apathy* means? Let me break it down for you: *a-pathos.* Without passion. Without love. In other words you're dead at the core. The fact is that if you really belong to Christ, the Spirit of God within you will not *allow* you to live like that. He will convict you out of your gourd. He'll put you through the wringer. The Spirit of God will make your life utterly miserable...until you repent.

> "I know your deeds; you have a reputation of being alive, but
> you are dead. Wake up! Strengthen what remains and is about

to die, for I have not found your deeds complete in the sight of my God." (Revelation 3:1b–2, NIV)

"Wake up!" the Lord tells this church. "Open your eyes before it's too late. Wake up before your lamp goes out and you have no witness left."

He says the same thing to you and me, doesn't He? If you want to change your Christian walk, you're going to have to wake up to certain facts. Number one, wake up to what you're doing wrong. Quit making excuses for it. Quit telling yourself it doesn't really matter, because it *does* matter very, very much. Wake up to the fact that there's a God who is willing to change you and mold you, but that you first need to open your eyes and get out of that prone position before you slip into a coma. Wake up to those personal habits that you know are not pleasing to God. Go ahead and confess them as sin and do something about them instead of continually justifying them.

Years before Jesus sent these letters to the churches in Asia, Paul gave the same kind of wake-up call to the believers in Rome and Ephesus.

And do this, knowing the time, that now it is high time to awake out of sleep; for now our salvation is nearer than when we first believed. The night is far spent, the day is at hand. Therefore let us cast off the works of darkness, and let us put on the armor of light. Let us walk properly, as in the day, not in revelry and drunkenness, not in licentiousness and lewdness, not in strife and envy. But put on the Lord

Jesus Christ, and make no provision for the flesh, to fulfill its lusts. (Romans 13:11–14)

"Wake up, O sleeper,
rise from the dead,
and Christ will shine on you."
(Ephesians 5:14b, NIV)

Wake up! It's *high time* (I like that) you were rollin' out of that bed. Climb out of that grave and shake off the dirt. Let the light of Christ shine on you so that you *catch fire.*

Have you ever been looking off to the west through your neighborhood when the sun comes up behind you? When the first rays of sun hit a window in the distance, that little square of glass just explodes with light. It changes from an ordinary window to a small replica of the sun. You can't even look at it anymore because the reflected glory is so intense it burns your eyes. That's what this verse makes me think of. Wake up, church, rise from the dead, and Christ will make you explode with His light and His glory.

The time to wake up is now.

The time to quit hitting the snooze button is now.

You know you're not studying the Word of God every day. *Wake up. Do it.*

You know you haven't spent five minutes in prayer in the last five days. *Get after it.* Seek Him now. He's right where you left Him.

You know you're not letting the Spirit of God control you. *Start now. Give up the steering wheel.* If you don't, you may die in what you are doing. You may sleepwalk through your years on earth and accomplish nothing for the King.

What's it like for you when that alarm clock goes off in the morning? Maybe you're like me, and it takes a few minutes for you to figure out if you're really alive or not. You know what I mean. *Am I alive or dead? Is this reality or a sequel to my last nightmare?* You've got to get yourself together, don't you? You've got to pry open those eyelids, get on your feet, splash a little cold water on your face, and smell the coffee.

That's what Jesus is saying here. Shake yourself out of dreamland before the whole day is past and it's night again. Get yourself together and get something done before it's too late.

Maybe you've been sleepwalking for quite a while, and you feel a little bit discouraged about that. You're wondering if you can still have much of an impact for Christ. You think that the church seems dead or irrelevant to most people anyway. But do you know what happens when something dead starts breathing? Trust me, Jack, it gets noticed.

ARISE FROM THE DEAD

I remember a time when someone rising from the dead just about finished *me* off! In our little town of Anniston, Alabama, the schools were segregated; kids from our neighborhood couldn't go to the school closest to our homes. Some of the kids rode a bus across town, but a number of us were too poor to ride the bus and had to walk from south Anniston out to the west part of town—nearly ten miles.

That's a long way to walk to school. In the morning you had to get up really early and flat get after it, or you'd never make it to class on time. In the afternoons, though, there was no rush. There could be up to one hundred black kids walking from west Anniston to south Anniston. Now when you have a bunch of kids all walking through the middle of town to get home, there are only two things that can happen: They can get in trouble, or they can get in trouble!

The shopkeepers always looked a little nervous when that mob of kids walked through. Let's go ahead and admit it (this was Alabama in the sixties): What do you think those downtown folks were saying to one another when we came through? "Watch it! They're gonna steal somethin'!"

And they were usually right!

Now, one of the best black-owned businesses in town was the Anniston Funeral Home. Ol' Lucius the mortician was the richest person in the black community because eventually everybody had to do business with him! So Lucius had a swank, luxurious place down-town—right in the path of our homeward journey. To break the monotony of our daily trek, several of us started visiting the mortuary on our way home.

Well, you know how that goes. If two or three kids will do it, it really catches on. So we started having a bunch of kids come by the mortuary every afternoon, causing a racket, making fun, cracking jokes, looking at the caskets, and generally being a nuisance.

After several days of this, Lucius got tired of it. It wasn't dignified having all those kids laughing and messing around in his establishment. So he decided to teach us a lesson. Lucius had one of his workers put on a suit and rub a little chalky powder on his face and hands. This black guy was looking pale! He climbed into one of the caskets, laid down in it, closed his eyes, and folded his hands across his chest. He looked more like a corpse than the real deal.

So here we came, doing our afternoon walk-through, and we saw this guy all laid out in one of the showrooms. "Oooh," someone said, "they've got a body in there!" Now that was just a little bit creepy, but I was the big athlete, right? I wasn't supposed to be afraid of anything. So we gathered around the open casket and checked this guy out.

I bent down to look into the face of this departed soul, and suddenly one of the eyelids flew open, and there was this eyeball staring at me. It was one of those times when you lean back to yell, but there's nothing there! I could only croak.

Then everybody started screaming and running for the door. The problem was that when the kids outside saw that there was something going on inside, they wanted to get in on the action. So we had a major tangle of bodies at the door. About that time those of us on the inside turned around to see that body climbing out of its casket. That did it. The inside group flattened the outside group and didn't look back. I made it home in record time that night. I may have even beaten the bus.

When a dead guy opens an eye and stares back at you, it gets your attention.

Hey, isn't it the same way with the church today? When society sees a church that they thought was dead open an eye to the truth, it shakes them up. When they see us climb out of our caskets and start living and breathing and walking again, people stop and look. So don't be discouraged that our culture considers the church dead and irrelevant. That's an advantage. When *life* arrives on the scene, nobody misses it! Be alive in Christ and watch what happens. You'll stand out like a former corpse taking laps around the mortuary, and you'll have an audience.

What's the first thing we've got to do if we're not going to be dead Christians or a dead church? We've got to wake up, throw off our sins and our old selfish habits, and let the light of Christ begin to shine out of the darkness like a sunrise.

You want to be righteous? By the power of the Holy Spirit, quit doing unrighteous things and start pursuing holiness.

You want to be loving? By the power of the Holy Spirit, quit doing things that are unloving and start loving.

You want to be like Christ? Then by the mighty power and control of God's Spirit, quit doing things Jesus would never do and start imitating Him.

"I KNOW YOUR WORKS"

"These things says He who has the seven Spirits of God and the seven stars: 'I know your works.'" (Revelation 3:1)

When Jesus Christ says He knows, He *knows*. This is the Word of God incarnate, the One who is living and powerful.

The Lord of the church says, "I am not satisfied with your phoniness. I am not impressed by your masquerade. I am not deceived by that thin glaze of holiness. I am not pleased with your exterior Christianity. And you'd better stop it right now!"

The problem with the Sardis church was that they pretended to be spiritual when they weren't. They were doing everything to make people think they were spiritual, but it was only window dressing. They were like one of those sets in the back lot of some Hollywood studio. You open the door to one of those beautiful, solid looking buildings and find yourself in a sandy weed patch. There's nothing there but an empty lot behind that great looking exterior. The Son of God knows this very well, and says, "I am not pleased with you."

And if He's not pleased with Christians in the church at Sardis pretending to be what they're not, how do you think He feels about you and me when we try the same thing? There is nothing more phony than phony righteousness or more hollow than hollow Christianity. Sardis might have looked good to the surrounding countryside; they might have looked good to other churches; they might have even looked good to themselves. They could have been involved in all kinds of righteous acts and charity bazaars and United Way campaigns. But they already had one foot in the grave.

Jesus arrived at their doorstep like a paramedic, ready to slap the paddles on their chest. "Remember therefore how you have received and heard; hold fast and repent" (Revelation 3:3). He was saying, "Listen, there's still an opportunity for you to turn around. There's still time for you to repent so that we can have fellowship again. Do it!" There was still time for one more "Hail Mary" shot at the end zone, but after that the clock would read 00:00. Game over.

Do you know anyone like Sardis: looking good on the outside but dead on the inside? Sardis was a church that didn't even know it was dead. It was a church living on its past accomplishments and newspaper clippings. It was a church that had a reputation for great preaching and teaching. But if there's one thing I learned in the National Football

League, it's that you can only live on your reputation so long. Maybe you were all-pro for seven straight years; maybe you had your mug on the cover of *Sports Illustrated* or on a box of Wheaties and are pretty impressed with yourself. The trouble is that the big rookie coming right out of college might not understand that he's supposed to hold you in awe. He might just knock you right on your can.

Sardis was feeling pretty good about themselves. They were at peace with the world. But peacefulness isn't necessarily a good thing. Graveyards are very, very peaceful. You can hear the wind rustling through the grass. (In Seattle, you can hear the rain dripping off the trees.) The reason it's peaceful in a graveyard is because there's an absence of life. When you're devoid of life there are no arguments, no controversies, no disagreements. Everything is calm and serene—quiet as a cemetery. Now there are two reasons why a church or a Christian might be peaceful: One, because you're right with God; or two, because you're dead!

God says, "I don't want you to be a dead sacrifice. I want you to be a living sacrifice." You put a dead sacrifice on the altar, and it just lays there. But you put a living sacrifice on the altar, and it starts squirming when the heat's on! You may start yelling, "Hey, this is gettin' hot! I want off!" And you've got to be committed to stay on that altar, endure the heat, and be that living sacrifice that is "holy and acceptable to God." Most Christians' commitment today is like the kamikaze pilot who flew thirty missions!

That's the church of Sardis. Resting on its laurels, on its history, and on its reputation in the community, but dead as a mackerel. Are you trying to rest on the laurels of:

- what you used to do for Christ?
- how you used to study?
- how you used to pray?
- how you used to lead others to Him?
- how you used to be so fired up and full of joy?

Are you doing absolutely nothing for the Lord but thinking about those "good ol' days"? You've got a positive exterior, but if someone put a stethoscope to your chest there'd be nothing there. The porch light's on, but there's nobody home.

Listen to the Lord of the church "who loved us and washed us from our sins in His own blood" (Revelation 1:5), and repent! Wake up! Climb out of that casket, and let Him shine on you. The world will stop in its tracks when it sees the dead walking.

STRENGTHEN WHAT REMAINS

"Be watchful, and strengthen the things which remain, that are ready to die, for I have not found your works perfect before God." (Revelation 3:2)

Waking up is step one. Admitting the condition of your heart and walking out the doors of that mortuary into the sunshine is a good first step. But then the Lord tells us to "strengthen the things which remain." One translation says, "Strengthen what little remains, for even what is left is at the point of death" (NLT).

In other words, there isn't a lot of time to mull this over. If the doctor tells you that you're on the verge of a massive heart attack and that your only hope is to start exercising, stop smoking, and stop eating Big Macs, then you'd better stuff those Marlboros down the garbage disposal, cook up some broccoli, and lace up those tennis shoes *now*.

How do we do that in the spiritual life? How do we strengthen ourselves when we've been sick and weak for years?

Confess your sin

If the Lord spoke words to Ken Hutcherson like He said to Sardis, I can tell you where I'd be: down on my face confessing every sin I could remember and even more that I couldn't. It starts with that word *R-E-P-E-N-T*. I wouldn't be getting up from my facedown position until I had done business with God.

The truth is, heaven's switchboard has an open line on His phone for repenting sinners. They get through every time. God hears the faintest cry and responds so fast it'll jerk your head around, Jack.

I can't help but think of King Manasseh in 2 Chronicles. He was the most despicable, evil king who ever ruled over Judah and Israel. He was kind of like Hitler and Stalin and Saddam Hussein all rolled into one ugly package. He trashed the temple of God, shed rivers of innocent blood, sacrificed his own sons in the fire, then "seduced Judah and the inhabitants of Jerusalem to do more evil than the nations whom the LORD had destroyed before the children of Israel" (2 Chronicles 33:9).

The Lord pleaded with Manasseh and his people to change their ways, but they totally shut their ears and wouldn't listen. Finally, God "brought upon them the captains of the army of the king of Assyria, who took Manasseh with hooks, bound him with bronze fetters, and carried him off to Babylon" (2 Chronicles 33:11). So there was Manasseh, clamped in rusty chains, cooling his heels in the sub-basement level of a Babylonian dungeon.

So what does this cat do? He cries out to God. This guy's got nerve! But that's not the amazing part. Who wouldn't cry out to God in a situation like that? To me the amazing part is that God listened to him.

> Now when he was in affliction, he implored the LORD his God, and humbled himself greatly before the God of his fathers, and prayed to Him; and He received his entreaty, heard his supplication, and brought him back to Jerusalem into his kingdom. Then Manasseh knew that the LORD was God. (2 Chronicles 33:12–13)

Yeah, I guess so! And listen, if God will hear the cry of a loser like Manasseh from the depths of a stinking dungeon in Babylon, if He can clean up a bloody dictator and restore him to dignity and honor, he can certainly hear you when you cry out for forgiveness and mercy in the mighty name of Jesus. If the believers at Sardis had cried out like that in the first century, we might still have a living, vibrant church in that place today, smack-dab in the middle of Turkey.

Get renewed in the Word

If I'd gotten this message from God, after confessing my sins I'd be pleading with the Lord to fill me with His Holy Spirit so that I would have the *power* to live a changed life. Growing in repentance, remember?

Paul has some good counsel for "strengthening what remains" in his words to the Romans:

> I beseech you therefore, brethren, by the mercies of God, that you present your bodies a living sacrifice, holy, acceptable to God, which is your reasonable service. And do not be conformed to this world, but be transformed by the renewing of your mind, that you may prove what is that good and acceptable and perfect will of God. (Romans 12:1–2)

You need to renew your mind by the Word of God so that you can walk in the way that is good, acceptable, and perfect. Am I going to do what is right, or am I going to do what is wrong? Am I going to follow my old ways, or do a one-eighty and walk that narrow path of righteousness? The more I mature, the more I stop picking the wrong and choose to do that which is better. As I do, evil begins to lose its grip on my life.

As I strengthen myself by being in the Word every day, the Holy Spirit comes into my life with His wisdom, discernment, power, and comfort. Comfort is not the absence of problems; comfort is the strength to face my problems.

Some of us will try to fool ourselves. We'll go two or three weeks without studying the Scriptures and tell ourselves, "I'm okay." But we are lying, and we are dying. Some of us may even go three or four months—or a year—without studying the Scriptures, and we still tell ourselves we're okay. It's a big lie. We're living a dead man's life, with only the faintest heartbeat to show we're alive at all.

Seek Christian fellowship

That's where true Christian fellowship steps in. That's where a brother or sister gets in your face and says, "What's going on here? Are you alive or are you dead? I know what 'dead' smells like, and I've got my concerns about you!"

Just the other day I heard a radio program about a guy in Germany who died in his little house while sitting on the couch. His corpse sat there almost eighteen months before anybody discovered it. This fellow lived alone and had cut off all contact with the only two people who might have cared about him: his ex-wife and his mother. So when he died, nobody missed him.

If you're part of a church that's alive and meeting with people who are alive, you're not going to be allowed to stay a corpse for long. They won't let you. They're going to challenge you and confront you and encourage you and love you back into the land of the living. Remember what it says in Hebrews: "Beware, brethren, lest there be in any of you an evil heart of unbelief in departing from the living God; but exhort one another daily, while it is called 'Today,' lest any of you be hardened through the deceitfulness of sin" (Hebrews 3:12–13).

Did you see that word *daily?* It means we need brothers and sisters exhorting us every day so that we don't find our hearts getting hard, so that we don't fall into the deceitfulness of sin. That means that if I'm your accountability partner, you will be getting a phone call or an e-mail from me every day. I'll be constantly checking in on your life—and you'll be doing the same with me. Who wants hardening of the heart? Who wants to depart from the living God? Who wants to climb back into the casket and close the lid? Not me. No, no. We need each other.

Keep watch!

Let me give you a little history of Sardis. I think it'll make Jesus' words come alive even more.

Sardis was set atop a spur of Mt. Tmolus. The Pactolus River ran around its base, making the city virtually impregnable. It was such a protected position that the city's defenders never bothered to guard it. So it was that a Median soldier scaled the wall like a thief in the night and allowed an attacking army inside. Such are the consequences of failing to watch. In A.D. 17 the city was destroyed by an earthquake. It was rebuilt quickly, but it never fully recovered. It had a reputation of being alive, but it was dead. The best anyone could do was strengthen what remained—and set a vigilant watch.

Now read Jesus' words:

"And to the angel of the church in Sardis write,

'These things says He who has the seven Spirits of God and the seven stars: "I know your works, that you have a name that you are alive, but you are dead. Be watchful, and strengthen the things which remain, that are ready to die, for I have not found your works perfect before God. Remember therefore how you have received and heard; hold fast and repent. Therefore if you will not watch, I will come upon you as a thief, and you will not know what hour I will come upon you."'" (Revelation 3:1–3)

Sardis would have felt a chill when they heard these words. You see, twice in their history they had been caught napping and had been invaded because a "thief in the night" had sneaked in from a direction they hadn't bothered to guard. For many years Sardis had been invincible—the strongest city in all the area. Had they begun to feel fat and sassy behind those city walls? Had they become complacent? Had they gotten caught up in the ancient versions of watching TV, cruising the Internet, and playing the Lotto?

Evidently something did happen, because at two separate times in their history, invaders had come like thieves in the night, broken through their defenses, and destroyed them. It happened first in the sixth century B.C. under Cyrus, king of the Persians. Three hundred years later they were defeated in exactly the same way by Antiochus the Great. Both times the invaders got in by sending someone up the side of an impossible hill. The folks in Sardis had drifted off to comfortable sleep and had awakened as prisoners—or hadn't awakened at all. All because they didn't set one guy up there to just look over that way.

So when Jesus talked about Sardis watching or else He would come like a thief in the night, they knew very well what He meant. The Lord deliberately used those shocking words to awaken them from their slumber. He was coming like a thief. He was coming in an hour when they didn't expect Him.

It's the same today. Jesus Christ *is* coming back. We need to wake up, strengthen ourselves, and live as though He were coming any minute.

I'll tell you this: When He comes, I don't want to be ashamed. I don't want Him to find me with my hand in the cookie jar. I don't want Him to find me in bed with another man's wife. I don't want Him to

SARDIS: ALMOST (BUT NOT QUITE) TERMINAL

find me with a cold, cynical heart, living like a walking corpse. I want to be ready. When that moment comes, when I hear the trumpet and the shout of the archangel, when I shoot up through Seattle's gray skies like a bottle rocket, I want one emotion in my heart, and I don't want it to be shame. I want to meet Him with a heart bursting with joy.

WALKIN' IN WHITE

"You have a few names even in Sardis who have not defiled their garments; and they shall walk with Me in white, for they are worthy." (Revelation 3:4)

I think it's a crack-up that all of us are going to be walking around in white! Praise be to God that the garments will be white, for we know people won't be worrying about color in heaven. The color of our garments or the color of our skin won't even be an issue. And if we know that's the way it's going to be in heaven, maybe we ought to start learning now how to live that way on earth—so the shock won't be too great!

Jesus the Bridegroom is waiting for His bride, the church. How is a bride dressed? In white, of course. Some of you may have forgotten why brides wear white! In today's society they wear white because it's a nice color and it looks great with whatever the bridesmaids are wearing. Who remembers anymore that white represents purity? Who remembers that a bride wearing white means she's saved herself for one man?

There's nothing more beautiful than a bride. Have you noticed that there's always a different response in the room when the bride starts down the aisle? When the groomsmen walk in, someone might whisper, "Nice suit," "Nice tux," or "When you consider what he has to work with, he's looking pretty good." The person commenting generally doesn't make a big deal over the groom and the groomsmen (unless she's a single lady!)

Then the bridesmaids come in, and what happens? Guys start looking at their watches, wondering, *When does this thing get over?* Most of the ladies are checking out the dresses, how the girls look, and giving their Kleenexes a workout.

Then in walks the bride, hanging on Daddy's arm.

The music swells. Everybody stands up. You hear the ahhs and oohs all over the room. *Isn't she beautiful?*

What do you think that bridegroom's doing? That boy's got goo-goo-gaa-gaa eyes. All he can see is a vision in white satin and lace. His heart starts pounding like he's just sprinted a hundred meters.

I remember how it was at my own wedding. I wanted two guys to escort my bride down the aisle so she wouldn't change her mind and run way. No, sir. This was the day we were going to say "I do!" And when she came down the aisle in lovely slow motion, I had to bite my tongue to keep from yellin', "She's *mine!* I'm *hers.* And in a few minutes we're gonna be *ours!* Here we go! Come on, girl, come on. I can't wait!" Talk about anticipation.

Now, can you imagine what it's going to be like when the bride of Christ is taken out of this sick, broken world to meet Jesus in the air? We're not going to walk down any aisle in slow motion. No way. We're going to fly in. We're going to shoot into His presence like a missile. What an entrance.

Maybe you don't feel very "white" in your soul right now. Maybe you feel like you're one of those people in Sardis who had "defiled their garments." That's the wonder of our Savior's blood, my friend: He can make your heart whiter than a thousand dry cleaners ever could. Remember what it says in the book of Isaiah?

"Come now, and let us reason together,"
Says the LORD,
"Though your sins are like scarlet,
They shall be as white as snow;
Though they are red like crimson,
They shall be as wool." (Isaiah 1:18)

Yes, there were a few in Sardis who kept their hearts pure and true for Jesus. Just like a bride who has purposefully maintained her purity, so there were a few in Sardis who deserved to wear white in the Lord's presence. God always has His remnant.

What about you? Have you washed your garments in the Savior's blood? Are you whiter than snow? I'm not asking if you don't sin anymore; I'm asking if you have repented and are walking in repentance. Are you keeping yourself from the deep sin all around you?

WRITE YOUR OWN ENDING

The church of Sardis was living on borrowed time. The glory of the past could carry them so far, but after a while any corpse will begin to stink. Some historians say the church here had a brief revival. There was a bishop of Sardis, Melito, who in the second century was known for his piety. But then the Christian witness in Sardis faded from history. Their lamp was extinguished. Their testimony was stilled. Peaceful as a graveyard. Darkness closed in over that part of the world, and it remains there to this day.

How different it could have been if that church had responded to the Lord with all its heart, soul, mind, and strength. He gave them the chance. He called them one last time. He wrote His love in a letter that has survived for two thousand years. But they closed their hearts, clung to their hypocrisy, and lost the chance to turn their world upside down.

I don't want to be like Sardis! I don't want to rest on what has been; I want to press on to what lies ahead. When He comes, I want to be alive. On fire. Strong in the Holy Spirit. This is no time to hang around the mortuary or take naps in a casket. It's time to come alive.

Listen. Can you hear those footsteps? The Bridegroom is right at the door!

CHAPTER SEVEN

Philadelphia:
A LITTLE STRENGTH
IS A GOOD THING

We crave security. It's one of those universal needs out there. This world is a big, bad place and doesn't care about us one bit.

Needs come.

Tragedies fall from a blue sky.

People leave, people change.

Finances dwindle (or drop through some crack in the ground).

Accidents jar their way into our lives.

Life is uncertain. Though we don't let ourselves think about it much, we know that any one of us is never more than a heartbeat away from instant death.

A few years ago, a middle-aged couple was driving along U.S. 97 in southern Oregon when a massive boulder rolled off the cliff above them and completely flattened their car. Just like that, life was over.

Only moments before, that husband and wife might have been enjoying a pleasant conversation, looking out at the sunset over Klamath Lake. And then—that's it, Jack. Maybe they'd gotten into an argument over some small, insignificant issue. The husband was just about to answer his wife when *wham!* the argument was over.

If I had to pick one word for life on this earth, I might pick *uncontrollable.*

Out of control.

Beyond our control.

It's not surprising, then, that we flock to anything that can make us feel secure. We like health insurance. We like security systems. We like airbags and antilock brakes. We like lifetime guarantees and escape clauses. Some of us like big, scary dogs. We like how the term *life insurance* makes us feel. We love having an overflowing bank account because we believe money can secure us on a level place.

The truth is, we feel powerless in this world. It's too big, too much, and sometimes we feel too small. We have little strength against everything that comes, and we'd like to change that situation if we could. But we're going to see in a minute that God wants us to have only a little strength.

A little strength? Isn't that crazy? I don't know about you, but if someone walked up and told me, "Hutch, you only have a little strength," I don't think I'd be too pleased. Hey, I'm a world-class athlete, chump. (Used to be, anyway.) But we're going to see Jesus *praising* a church because it had only a little strength. How can that be? Keep reading.

We don't like to feel weak, do we? We want to feel strong and secure. To capture a feeling of security, we're willing to give up a lot. Let me illustrate with a story.

Let's say a single young man walks up to a single young woman and says something like this: "Hey, girl, I am the best thing for you. I want you to know what I say is the truth, and if you're with me you can never ever be bad. If you just listen to what I say, you will be the most secure woman in all the world, because I am the man!"

Now, that single lady is going to respond in one of two ways. She's either going to think, *That's an egotistical idiot right there!* or she's going to think, *Hmm, if he can back that up, I'd better get to know him. And I don't care how he looks!*

Is that a shock, that a woman wouldn't care about good looks if a man could make her feel secure? It shouldn't be. Let me tell you, when I was in football I saw some of the ugliest athletes with some of the finest looking women you'll ever see. Why? It wasn't because of how the athletes looked; it was because of their wallets.

True, those women might've just been gold diggers. But they also might've been attracted to men they thought could make them feel secure. They might've just been trying to meet that basic desire to feel safe, away from the edge of fear and poverty and disaster.

I'm here to tell you that a woman will put up with a lot of things in a man, even a dog-ugly face, if he can make her feel secure. I know that personally, because...because I do a lot of counseling! Ha—you didn't think I was going to take myself that low, did you?

The deepest desire in every human heart is the desire to be safe. That's what parents are there for. That's what mothers and especially fathers are there for: to keep that little baby safe. As we grow, we start to need another kind of security: eternal security.

Praise God, that's what our heavenly Father is there for! He holds the key to our eternal security.

HAVE YOU SEEN MY KEYS?

Whoever holds the keys is the person with the power, am I right? Everybody waits at the door until the guy with the key gets there, right? You send someone out looking for the custodian to get the key for the gym. Everybody panics when they see the keys dangling from the ignition inside the locked car. The best and worst sounds in a prison have to do with keys: Locked in or safely locked out, both require keys.

Remember that movie *ET*? For the longest time the only thing we ever saw of this one dude was the key chain dangling off his belt loop. Who was this key guy? The more we saw it, the more we felt he was a bad guy. The keys started standing for some kind of corrupt authority that wanted to lock our ugly alien away.

Keys represent control, power, and authority. He who holds the keys can open doors that no one else can open, and what he shuts no one but him can get back into.

I'm here to tell you that Jesus is the great Locksmith. Take a look:

"And to the angel of the church in Philadelphia write,

'These things says He who is holy, He who is true, "He who has the key of David, He who opens and no one shuts, and shuts and no one opens": I know your works. See, I have set before you an open door, and no one can shut it.'" (Revelation 3:7–8a)

Jesus is the man. He's in charge. He holds the only key. When He locks the thing, it's good and locked. When He opens it and wedges it open, there's no force in the universe that's going to pull it closed; it's not coming shut until He comes and does it Himself.

Who is this Man who can open what no one can open and shut what no one can shut? Who is this Man who can tell me what I can do? Who is this Man who can tell me what I can think? Who is this Man who can tell me whom I can marry? Who is this Man who can tell me what to do after I get married? Who is this Man who thinks He has that kind of control over me?

He is the great Locksmith, and I want to be on His side because His name is holy and true and He holds the key of David.

Any idea what this key of David idea is about? We get some background on this from the book of Isaiah. God's basically firing a dude named Shebna for being unworthy to hold the key to the treasury, and He's about to install a guy named Eliakim in his place:

The key of the house of David
I will lay on his shoulder;
So he shall open, and no one shall shut;
And he shall shut, and no one shall open.
(Isaiah 22:22)

The key of David is talking about God's authority. It means, "Only I have the right to override My character, which I won't. And since I'm not going to override it, no one else can reach in and unlock your relationship with Me."

Suppose I gave you the key to my front door. "Use it anytime you want," I say because we're so tight. Now wouldn't that be something to give you the authority to come into my house anytime you want? But let's say I forget to mention one thing. Let's say I gave you the key to my front door but I didn't tell you about my rottweilers roaming loose on my property. The question is, would you ever *make* it to my front door?

Let me tell you something. There are a lot of us that will open our lives to one another, especially in families, but that always keep something locked away and hidden. Isn't that right? We trick each other in relationships. We don't ever become fully vulnerable to each other. We've got that little hidden part of us that we hide away. Why? Because we don't completely trust people—not even family. There is always this fear that the other person is going to find out what that hidden thing is. But we don't want anybody to know *that*. So we lock it up, hide it under the bed, and throw away the key.

Sometimes we try to do that with God. We think we're going to give His Holy Spirit access to parts of our life, but not all. We think we can keep a few choice things hidden away from His searching eye.

But Jesus says, "I've got the key of David. And every one of your thoughts, your emotions, and your secrets are unlocked to me, Jack. I can open them, view them, explore them, and shout them out from the rooftops. Do you think you are so sneaky and careful that no one can ever find out what's in that lockbox of your heart? Not a chance! I have the key of David."

Jesus doesn't just hold the key; He *is* the key. Anything He wants to do with you, He can do. He can open any door or close it, and when

He opens it, it can't be closed. When He closes it, all the wishing in the world won't open it. You can have more faith than Van de Kamps has pork and beans, but it won't mean anything when He shuts that door.

KEYS ALSO OPEN GATES

Back in the first century A.D., a little town named Philadelphia knew all about opening and closing. The town was known as the "gateway to the east" (not to be confused with Ephesus, the gateway to Asia), and its whole purpose was to put the lockdown treatment on another culture.

Philadelphia was the youngest town of the seven in Revelation 2–3. It was established in 189 B.C. as a missionary town. I wish I could tell you it was a missionary town for God, but it wasn't. It was founded to expand the presence of Greek philosophy and language in the area and to crush the philosophy and language of a former empire, Lydia.

The name *Philadelphia,* as you may know, means the city of brotherly love. *Philos* means fond affection, and *adephos* means a brother. So Philadelphia literally means a brother's fond affection. It comes from the nickname of the man who founded the city. Atalla II was king of Pergamum when he got this town up and running. His brother, Eumenes, was so fond of Atalla that he gave him the nickname, Philadelphus—a brother's love. And Atalla gave that name to the town he started.

Nice to have a friendly name for a city with such a cruel purpose, isn't it?

Did you know that Philadelphia is still a living city to this day? Almost thirty thousand people live there. These days it's called Alasehir.

Would you believe there's still a Christian presence there? Despite centuries of Turkish influence, Ottoman rule, and Muslim pressure, five Christian churches remain in this town.

Why? Because when God opens a door, no one can shut it but Him. When God is pleased with you, as He was with Philadelphia, He sustains you. The churches at Philadelphia, my church and your church, believers in the world, and the church of God itself—will all remain in this world so long as Christ is pleased with us and has need of us.

THE ULTIMATE DOOR

Is there any good door, any good opportunity, or any good treasury that you can get to without God opening it to you? Is there anyone who can take from you the opportunity God gives? If you give something to God to keep, how safe is it? If God is guarding someone, how vulnerable is he?

Opportunities and promises are safe in God's care. But when He who is holy and true spoke of the key of David in this passage, I think He was talking about something else that can never be revoked: our salvation.

Let's talk about eternal security, all right? Some people don't want me to talk about it. They say, "Oh, Hutch, that makes people lazy. If they feel they can never lose something, why should they work for it?" I think those people are getting God mixed up with welfare! You see, when God lets you know that you cannot lose what He has given you, it sets you free to love Him instead of trying to make Him love you.

My wife knows that I am totally committed to her. She knows that there is absolutely nothing she could ever do to make me stop loving her. Why? Because my love for her is not based upon what she does. It's based on my commitment. She knows that I would go one-on-one with a Mack truck for her. She knows that for a fact. She doesn't have to guess. She doesn't have to wonder.

And listen…knowing that *sets her free.*

See, she knows she can commit the worst sins in her life against me, she can hurt me deeply, but one thing she never ever has to worry about is me up and leaving her. She knows that I will always, always take her back. So she can relax and get on with living and loving.

Now, if a human man can give that kind of committed love, what kind of love do you think the great Bridegroom has for His bride? Let me ask you: How bad do you think you have to be to make Him stop loving you? Worse than you *can* be, my friend, worse than you can ever be.

CAN I GET EIGHT WITNESSES?

Jesus holds the key to salvation. He has set an open door before us, and I for one have walked through. Now that I'm on the other side of that decision, my salvation is locked away safe and secure in heaven's treasury.

Have you believed? Is He reigning in your heart? If so, you can just forget about Him leaving you, because He won't. Know how I know? I know that you and I have eternal security because of eight things that flow from our blessed Redeemer. My salvation is secure because of the Savior's blood, Word, power, hand, prayer, life, love, and seal.

The Savior's blood

The first reason I know my salvation is safe and eternal is that it's based on the blood of Jesus Christ, the Messiah.

> Christ came as High Priest of the good things to come, with the greater and more perfect tabernacle not made with hands, that is, not of this creation. Not with the blood of goats and calves, but with His own blood He entered the Most Holy Place once for all, having obtained eternal redemption. (Hebrews 9:11–12)

Jesus Christ, the Man of all men, says, "I went into the holy of holies to shed My blood for you, once and forever, and I obtained eternal redemption for you."

Now, how good is the blood of Christ? It is perfect, right? It is forever. Do you realize that if you believe you can lose your salvation, you have called Christ's blood weak? You have said it's only purchased a temporary redemption, something that needs constant updating and renewing. You have trampled the Son of God underfoot, counted the blood of the covenant by which you were sanctified a common thing, and insulted the Spirit of grace (Hebrews 10:29).

I don't know about you, but I know God the Father well enough to know He'd never allow His Son to come to this earth and die for you and me and shed His blood for a temporary salvation. His blood purchased an eternal salvation.

The Savior's Word

God's Word is eternal, amen? He said it; I believe it; that settles it. Until heaven and earth pass away, not one jot or tittle will pass away until it's all fulfilled. If you believe that, then you have to believe that what God says is eternally true, right?

Careful, now, I'm a trickster. You may find yourself skewered on your own objections.

If God's Word is eternal and true, then this is eternal and true, too:

> "Most assuredly, I say to you, he who hears My word and believes in Him who sent Me has everlasting life, and shall not come into judgment, but has passed from death into life." (John 5:24)

How clear is *that*? Clear as a summer sky in Montana. Clear as a trout stream in Alaska. The only way that statement could ever be cloudy or muddy is if you deliberately made it cloudy or muddy.

If you want to know what Jesus thinks about this issue, check out what He says. He has written it down. "If you hear My word and believe in Me, *you have eternal life right now*. Any questions?"

What does eternal life mean? Can you really have eternal life temporarily? It can't be sort of eternal or partially eternal or kind of eternal. It's either eternal or it's temporary, either infinite or finite. What does God think? He thinks it's eternal. That's what His Word says. Therefore the person who teaches that you can lose your salvation is calling Jesus Christ a liar.

Too strong? "Oh, Hutch, you can't say that." No? Is this how it is, then—Jesus said it; I don't believe it; that settles it? If you think you can lose your salvation, shame on you! You are calling Jesus Christ a liar. Face the facts; they're right in front of you. Why discuss it when He who never lies has told you something?

He says, "I am holy and I am *true*. I have passed from death into life." My eternity is secure because the One who holds the keys says it is.

The Savior's power

Do you know how I know I'm gloriously saved and don't even worry about it? Because the power of God is holding together what the Lord Jesus Christ won for me at Resurrection Day.

> Blessed be the God and Father of our Lord Jesus Christ, who according to His abundant mercy has begotten us again to a living hope through the resurrection of Jesus Christ from the dead, to an inheritance incorruptible and undefiled and that does not fade away, reserved in heaven for you, who are kept by the power of God through faith for salvation ready to be revealed in the last time. (1 Peter 1:3–5)

I don't worry about my salvation because my inheritance is reserved. It's safe in heaven, locked away by the key of David in God's treasury, incorruptible and unfading, waiting for little ol' me to get in there and unwrap my presents. It's kept there by the power of God. Not my power to obey God or sacrifice to God or even always to love serving God. But by His power.

Do we even have to talk about how strong God's power is? Do I have to ask what it would take to overthrow God's power so that a thief could get in there and walk out with my salvation tucked under his coat? Good. Because if you think God is a liar who isn't powerful enough to keep your inheritance safe, then there's no reason to believe in Him at all. Right? Why believe in Him at all? Might as well eat, drink, and be merry, for tomorrow you burn like a Jimmy Dean pure pork sausage!

The Savior's hand

Ever try taking candy from a baby? Well, it might be as easy as people always say, but I'm here to tell you that once you get it you don't want it. It's all slimy and sticky and nasty. And that baby looks at you with that slippery grin, and you think, *Here, kid, take it back.*

Try taking my salvation out of Jesus' hand. Just try. No sir. That ain't happenin'.

> "My sheep hear My voice, and I know them, and they follow Me. And I give them eternal life, and they shall never perish; neither shall anyone snatch them out of My hand. My Father, who has given them to Me, is greater than all; and no one is able to snatch them out of My Father's hand." (John 10:27–29)

I'm going to get all theological on you for a minute. Pull out your Bible dictionaries and your Greek lexicons. Are you ready? Okay, here goes: Do you know what *never* means in Greek? There's a Greek word behind the English word *never* in that passage you just read: "They shall never perish." Here's a bit of Bible trivia with which you can amaze your friends and neighbors. The Greek word behind *never* in this passage literally means...never. N-E-V-E-R.

Fooled you, didn't I? Never means never. What does it mean in Swahili? *Never*. Russian? *Never*. In French, Cantonese, Spanish, Flemish, Setswana, and pig Latin, *never* means *never*. I don't care what language it is, He has given us a promise: You will never perish. What a glorious Lord we have!

Now let's look at the snatching part. Who can snatch Jesus' sheep from His hand? No one. Who can snatch them out of His Father's hand? No one. Really? So if I say I can lose my salvation, I'm saying that God almighty is like that gooey-fingered baby who couldn't hold onto his soul if eternity depended on it.

Well, Hutch, when you put it that way....

God says you are His—gloriously His. No one is going to take you because no one can. Not only does Jesus hold you in His hand, but on top of His hand is the hand of the Father, who has all power. We are good and saved, my brothers and sisters. Do you understand me? We are good and saved!

The Savior's prayer

I know my soul is eternally secure because Jesus prayed for it to be so.

> "Father, I desire that they also whom You gave Me may be with Me where I am, that they may behold My glory which You have given Me; for You loved Me before the foundation of the world." (John 17:24)

Search the Bible and see if you can find a place where Jesus' prayer was not granted. Go ahead.

"Lazarus, come forth." Granted.

"Rise up and walk." Granted.

"Let your eyes be opened." Granted.

"Wind and waves, be still." Granted.

What about Gethsemane? Maybe you're saying, "Jesus' prayer, 'Remove this cup from Me,' wasn't answered in the Garden of Gethsemane." Oh, but that was not the end of His prayer, was it? How did that prayer end? "Not My will but Your will." And *that* prayer was granted.

Do you know what you've got to say if you believe you can lose your salvation? You can't beat around the bush; you can't use spiritual jargon; you can't do your fancy dance. If you say you can lose your salvation, you've got to say that Jesus' prayer wasn't effective. Call it what it is: Jesus prayed for something but didn't receive it.

Are you ready to say that?

John tells us that every prayer prayed according to God's will is granted (5:14–15). So if we receive whatever we ask in Jesus' name, how powerful are Jesus' own prayers? I mean, who knows God's will better than Jesus Christ? So every one of His prayers, including the one to bring us to glory with Him, will be granted.

My eternity is safe because of the Savior's prayer.

The Savior's life

Ooh, how about the Savior's death and resurrection?

For if when we were enemies we were reconciled to God
through the death of His Son, much more, having been reconciled, we shall be saved by His life. (Romans 5:10)

This is one of those truths about God that just blows my little man
brain. Why in the world would God the Father decide that it was a good
idea to sacrifice God the Son for a bunch of stiff-necked, hard-hearted
hoodlums who always went their own way? I mean, would I ever sacrifice my own child to ransom a pack of murderers, adulterers, rebels, and
witches? Forget it, Jack. Let 'em fry. I'm keeping my child close to me.

If God will lay down His life when none of us wants Him, what
will happen to you and me when we belong to Him? What kinds of
relationships will that produce? Do you honestly think God Almighty
would let His Son die for you to go to hell?

Your salvation is secure because the Messiah laid down His life for
you—and because He rose to eternal resurrection. Yes, you are eternally secure.

The Savior's love

The security of your salvation rests neither with you nor with your love
for God, but with His love for you.

"Greater love has no one than this, than to lay down one's life
for his friends." (John 15:13)

I do a lot of counseling. You wouldn't believe some of the things I
hear. And you know me; I'm a speak-my-mind kind of guy. I like to get

in people's faces and tell them the hard truth and nothin' but the truth. But you can't do that in counseling. You have to be sensitive.

I have seen some dogs walk into my office, some serious dogs— both male and female. I'm constantly amazed, though, when these guys or girls will leave and do all kinds of things to hurt their mates, and those mates will still want 'em back. Sometimes I have to button my lip. Why? Because I just want to stand up and say, "You know what? This jerk isn't worth it. Pack up the kids and move out, honey." Or "After what that woman did to you you still want her back? What's wrong with you, Jack?" Oh, yes. That would make me feel real good. (For a minute. Then my counseling days would be over.)

There's one thing I've learned from these people: Love isn't about feelings—because I can tell you that their feelings are like roadkill on the superhighway of life—it's about commitment. I don't care how low or bad the other person is, what holds the spouse in that relationship is that she has committed to love that dog no matter what.

Now I want to ask you something. If imperfect women and men can still love spouses who have dissed them, what does God's perfect love do? How many times will God's perfect love forgive? How long will God's perfect love wait for that prodigal to come home?

Jesus Christ laid down His life for you and me.

That's how much He loves us.

He didn't do that lightly.

He didn't do it to give us a temporary eternal life.

I know I have eternal security because Jesus' love overflows for eternity and because He wouldn't give His life to achieve something that wasn't going to be permanent.

The Savior's seal

Have you ever gotten home from the grocery store and tried to open one of those vacuum-sealed packages? I think somebody invented those for the sole purpose of irritation!

Now, I'm from the South. Down south we love our bologna. We do. There is nothing in the world like bustin' open a fresh package of bologna. Ahh, that fragrance just fills the room, doesn't it? I love coming home from a hard day of staff meetings and counseling and sermon writing, opening that refrigerator, and finding a fresh package of Oscar Meyer's finest.

But then I get to working on that package, and I'm telling you, those things are locked tight. Those people weren't kidding around when they said they wanted to keep the freshness in and the other stuff out. Well, I'm the other stuff! That bologna is sealed, Jack! You get that knife and have at it, but it's no good. Your hand's lacerated in half a dozen places, there's blood everywhere, and your wife is calling 9-1-1. But that bologna is still vacuum sealed!

Let me tell you something: That's nothing compared to the seal that Jesus Christ puts on you when you come to Him in faith.

> In Him you also trusted, after you heard the word of truth, the gospel of your salvation; in whom also, having believed, you were sealed with the Holy Spirit of promise. (Ephesians 1:13)

You think God is going to allow His Holy Spirit to come and take residence in something He can't preserve?

Do you know what *sealed* means? It means finished. A finished transaction. It means ownership. You are owned; you were bought with a price. God took the contract to heaven and locked it in the safe. Tell me, can anyone reach into heaven and revoke that contract? No. Sealed means security. That's why we call it eternal security. Eternally sealed, bought and paid for. Transaction finished.

You are sealed if you're a Christian. Nobody can break that. If you can't get in a bologna package you can't break the seal of the Holy Spirit.

FINAL WITNESS

I know I'm saved, gloriously saved. How do I know I'm saved? Because I love Jesus and Jesus loves me. Jesus loves me, this I know, for the Bible tells me so. I am gloriously saved, wonderfully saved, beautifully saved, and glorified to the max because God loves me. I'm not going to lose my salvation, and I'm not going to waste my time thinking about it.

So if you and I can learn that God will never leave us, we can quit jumping through hoops trying to keep Him in love with us or impressed with us or thinking we're worthy of being kept. If He's committed to us in the way I've just described, we don't have to go on two-year pilgrimages to win favor before the Lord. We don't have to make all these sacrifices of volunteer work or teaching Sunday school or going on mission trips to keep the Lord in love with us or to hold on to our salvation.

When we realize our eternity is secure, we are set free from trying to keep His love and can move on to learning how to please Him who has showered us with His love.

FIGHTIN' WORDS

Let's get back to Philly, all right? In His letter to the church in Philadelphia, Jesus gives us the secret to pleasing God. That's what we want to do, right—please God? We're done with trying to hold on to Him and now we just want to serve Him out of gratitude and love. Well, here it is. But if you're like me, when you first hear it, you won't think it's a very good plan:

> "I know your works. See, I have set before you an open door,
> and no one can shut it; for you have a little strength, have kept
> My word, and have not denied My name." (Revelation 3:8)

There it is, that "little strength" thing. Still sounds like an insult, doesn't it? But it looks to me like Jesus means it as a compliment. What's going on here?

Like so much else, God doesn't see strength the way we see strength. He doesn't value it the way the world values it. If you see this statement from the world's perspective, it's a cut. If you see it from God's perspective, it's one of the highest compliments you could ever receive. Here He has set before the church at Philadelphia an open door of opportunity, and the first reason He gives for that is that they possess only a little strength.

The secret to pleasing God is to have only a little strength. Why? Because a little strength in yourself leaves room for a lot of strength in God.

Remember what it says in Psalms?

He does not delight in the strength of the horse;
He takes no pleasure in the legs of a man.
The LORD takes pleasure in those who fear Him,
In those who hope in His mercy.
(Psalm 147:10)

Jesus doesn't want you strong in yourself. No, no, no, no. God-dependence will never begin in your life until self-dependence dies.

He said to me, "My grace is sufficient for you, for My strength is made perfect in weakness." Therefore most gladly I will rather boast in my infirmities, that the power of Christ may rest upon me. Therefore I take pleasure in infirmities, in reproaches, in needs, in persecutions, in distresses, for Christ's sake. For when I am weak, then I am strong. (2 Corinthians 12:9–10)

If you want to please God, have a little strength.

By the way, if you're feeling full of yourself right now, you're probably not too dependent upon God. If you're His child and you're feeling this way, watch out: He's going to make you weak. That sounds wrong, doesn't it? But I'm here to tell you that God making you weak is an act of love. Why? Because He can't use you when you're full of yourself. If you want to be used by God—and you do, don't you?—you have to be weak. Sometimes you can choose weakness on your own. Sometimes He forces you into it. Either way, He's going to use you, and He's going to get the glory. One's just easier on the hide than the other.

STRENGTH IN WEAKNESS

There are two great things that having little strength will do for you: It will keep you humble and it will drive you to God.

First, if you've got only a little strength, you usually won't find yourself boasting all over the place. God values humility. It's a huge part of His character. Did you know that God is humble? Yes, He is. Holy God in a manger? That's humility, my friend. Let me tell you, God will change the direction of a nation for one righteous, humble man or woman.

God says, "I'll put you in a position where you've got a little strength, where you'll have to trust Me, because when you have to trust Me, you are humbled, and when you are humbled, you are My kind of person—one I can use tremendously."

Are you happy yet? Are you encouraged that God wants you weak and humbled? Do you have a good God or what?

Second, having little strength will drive you to God. When the onslaught comes, your strength is quickly overwhelmed, amen? To whom do all people, not just Christians, cry out when their own strength is overpowered? To God. That's why there are very few atheists in cancer wings and critical care units. That's why even pagans cry out, "Oh, my God!" when tragedy strikes. When human strength is used up and corporate strength has vanished and the wisdom of doctors is depleted and the power of technology is gone, what's left to cling to? *Anything* that makes you pray.

Do you believe that?

No matter how degrading it is, how hurtful it is, or how tough it is, if it drives you to God, if it pushes you hard into His arms, then it is a blessing. I believe with all my heart that most of the problems that come into our lives are meant to drive us to God. I mean, look at Paul. If he hadn't been given his thorn in the flesh, whatever it was, he wouldn't have cried out to God about it—and we would've been without one of the most profound truths in the Bible.

Your problems, your weaknesses, your infirmities, your poverty—whatever it is that drives you to cry out to God is, in some sense, a good thing. God wants us dependent because humble, empty, down-and-out people that don't trust in themselves are the ones He can use.

When you're a Christian, hitting bottom isn't such a bad thing. The bottom is solid! It doesn't give. *You can't get any lower than the palm of His hand.* What a great place to push off from; what a great foundation to build on! Jesus Christ wants to teach you the secret to accessing God's power...and the secret to that power is weakness.

Picture a glass that's half-full of water (I'm an optimist, see?). Now put a lid over the top. The water is your strength, and the air is God's strength. The more water that's in there, the less air there is. The more self-sufficient you are, the less God-dependent you are. But that empty glass with only a drop swishing around in the bottom, man, that thing's *full* of air.

If I have to be empty of myself to be full of God's power, then bring it on! You may find yourself praying something you can't believe you're saying: *God, please make me a person of little strength!*

A little is a lot

The good news is that "a little strength" is all you need. With a little strength you can overcome a lot of bad. A little strength is all you need to obey God in the moment. If you've got a little strength, you can say no to things that could lead you into years of sin.

Now, way back when I was a studly kind of guy, when I was single and a young Christian, sometimes I'd be walking down the street and here would come one of these fine little fillies! We're talking about a fine little filly from the Wild Willy Filly Club! She would come up and say, "Hey, how are you doing, big boy? Let's go out." And I'd go, "No!"

I didn't beat around the bush like some folks like to do: "Well, you know, she *is* good-looking. There could be a possibility here. I don't want to turn her off to Christ, you know."

No sir. I'd summon up just a little bit of strength, and I'd say no. With a little strength, I saved myself from maybe a whole life of going out with that girl of sin. Just a little strength overrides a lot of wrong.

A little strength says, "I know I need to witness to this person, but you know, he really doesn't want to hear it. He doesn't want me to say anything to him." Just a little strength overrides that fear and helps me say, "I want to tell you about Jesus Christ." That little bit of strength may lead him into accepting Jesus Christ. And then angels will be doing flips, all because of your little strength.

ARE YOU STILL HERE?

God sustains those He's pleased with. That's the lesson from the church at Philadelphia. There is no word of rebuke in Jesus' letter to this church. He finds no fault in them. He sets a permanently open door in front of them: a door of opportunity, a door of influence, and a door of salvation.

"Because you have kept My command to persevere, I also will keep you from the hour of trial which shall come upon the whole world, to test those who dwell on the earth. Behold, I come quickly! Hold fast what you have, that no one may take your crown." (Revelation 3:10–11)

The church in Philadelphia persevered. They clung to God with what little strength they had. They took advantage of the opportunity God had given them by placing them at the gateway to the east. And so God promised to spare them from the tribulation that was coming upon the earth.

There was a Cary Grant/Katharine Hepburn movie made in 1940 called *The Philadelphia Story.* This movie was put together over sixty years ago, but it's still kickin' around on late-night cable.

There is also a *real* Philadelphia Story. The church in Philadelphia—the one Jesus spoke to over two thousand years ago—is still here today. Why? Because God is pleased with them, and He's still got a purpose for them. He's seen no reason to rebuke them, so they have been miraculously preserved. So long as He's pleased with them, they will remain. No one shuts that door except the one with the key of David.

It's the same with the church in the world. Though five-sevenths of the church of today receives rebuke (Jesus chastises five of the seven churches of Revelation 2–3), still we're hanging on. God has something He wants to do with His church, and until that purpose is accomplished, the church is going to be here.

It's no different for you and me. If we're still here, it's because He's still got a purpose for us in this world. Do you know what your purpose is? Are you gettin' after it? What about this: Are you saved? Are you gloriously signed, sealed, and delivered? Are you enjoying the same eternal security I'm enjoying? Are you set free to quit worrying about keeping God? Have you moved on to learning how to please Him?

If you don't know how He wants you to live in order to please Him, just ask. If you want to know what God thinks, He's the one to go to. He'll show you. And I'll give you a hint: It's going to involve your being weak so He can be strong.

CHAPTER EIGHT

Laodicea:
NEITHER HOT
NOR COLD

You make me sick!

If you ever hear words like that, it's a pretty good clue you're in some kind of trouble. If you're making someone sick, you've gone beyond just annoying him or bothering him or disturbing him. Right? The very sight of you is making this person want to reverse the eating process. That's bad!

Husband, if you hear those words from your wife, you've got a lot of ground to make up. There's big trouble in the love nest.

If you hear those words from your employer, you'd better have that résumé tuned up, because you're history, Jack!

If you're standing before a judge and hear those words before the sentencing, you'd best not make any plans for the next ten years.

If you hear those words from your pastor, hang on to your chair. You're about to get sermonized!

You make me sick!

Those are strong words. We don't say those words to anybody unless we're very, very upset—almost at the end of our rope. We may *feel* sick because of something that's happened in your life, but most of us don't put it into words.

When I was playing football, sometimes I felt sick if we lost a close game—especially if I'd missed some key tackles. I've felt sick when a business deal went south after a lot of hard work. I've felt sick over blatant racial prejudice. In the ministry, I've felt sick over the hardness of people's hearts. It's the way you feel when someone you love and trust suddenly turns against you and begins acting like an enemy.

You feel it! It's like a big, cold rock sitting in the pit of your stomach.

But think about this: As bad as it would be to hear those words from your spouse or your boss or your pastor or your friend, how much worse it would be to hear them from the Son of God! Can you even imagine what it would be like to make God sick?

The church at Laodicea didn't have to imagine it, because they *heard* it—straight from Jesus Christ.

TROUBLE WITH A CAPITAL *T*

I'm here to tell you: The church in Laodicea was in big-time trouble. It's the only one of the seven churches addressed in Revelation 2–3 that doesn't get any praise from the Lord. To this church, the Lord has nothing good to say.

Now, you know that Jesus likes to start out His letters with good news. So if the one who was before *before* and after *after* searches your heart and can't find one good thing to say about you, you know you're in for it. It was all He could do just to talk to them at all. (But even here He brings hope—the most tender message of hope spoken to any of the seven.)

Even to Sardis, with all their problems, the Lord could say, "Strengthen the things that remain" and "You have a few folks who have not defiled their garments."

Not in Laodicea. To this church God said, "I'm about to vomit you out of My mouth." Ooh, that's harsh. That's a pretty strong rebuke. But it gets worse.

When I preached a series of messages on these seven churches, I showed slides of the ruins of each of these cities. I'd taken some of the pictures myself on our tours of the area. But when we came to Laodicea, guess what? There weren't any slides to show; we had to put up an artist's conception of the city on the screen. Why? Because God wiped it out, buried it, and it has never been dug up. Yes, the location of Laodicea has been pinpointed accurately, but the site has never been excavated. The entire city molders beneath the turf in western Turkey. The only visible remains are a few large, cut stones.

Contrast that with Philadelphia, which remains to this day: five Christian churches in Philadelphia. Why? Because when God's pleased with you, He miraculously sustains you. But when He's displeased...well, when He's displeased, all we can show of you is an artist's conception.

Christ told the Laodicean church He was about to spit them out of His mouth so they would no longer be useful, and that's exactly what happened. The church disappeared, and so did the city where they had been appointed to carry forth the Word of Life. Darkness descended over that area of the world and remains to this day. Christ still has His people in that place—He still has a remnant who have not bowed the knee to Allah. But the lampstand that once shone so brightly on that high mountain pass is gone.

Laodicea—the richest of all the seven cities mentioned in Revelation 2–3—was by all accounts a beautiful place. It was a town with a going church, too—a strong witness for Jesus Christ in a strategic corner of the world. With such strong advantages and blessings, how could things go so wrong?

That's an important question for all of us, isn't it?

THE LOST EPISTLE

Laodicea was part of a tri-city arrangement that is mentioned elsewhere in the Bible. When Paul wrote to the church at Colosse, he mentioned the neighboring towns of Hierapolis and Laodicea in the fertile Lycus valley (Colossians 4:13). The great Roman highway stretching to the interior of Asia from the coast at Ephesus ran straight through downtown Laodicea—a great place for a McDonald's franchise!

The fourth chapter of Colossians seems to hint that this dude Epaphras may have been one of the founding teachers, maybe even the head pastor, of the church of Laodicea. So they had a solid foundation and beginning. Epaphras came to Paul and gave him a good report about the church in Colosse. And when Paul wrote back to the church, he mentioned their pastor:

Epaphras, who is one of you, a servant of Christ, greets you, always laboring fervently for you in prayers, that you may stand

perfect and complete in all the will of God. For I bear him witness
that he has a great zeal for you, and those who are in Laodicea, and
those in Hierapolis.… Greet the brethren who are in Laodicea,
and Nymphas and the church that is in his house. Now when this
epistle is read among you, see that it is read also in the church of
the Laodiceans, and that you likewise read the epistle from
Laodicea. (Colossians 4:12–13, 15–16)

What's this? Paul says that the Colossians ought to get the letter he
sent to the Laodiceans and have it read in their church. Say what?
Search every Bible you can find, and unless it's some kind of "enhanced
by special revelation" Bible, you're not going to find Paul's letter to the
Laodiceans. *Jesus'* letter to the Laodiceans, yes. But Paul's, no. Where is
that letter?

Most likely, the apostle wrote that letter about the same time he
wrote to the Colossians, around A.D. 60. The book of Revelation was
written thirty-five years later, in A.D. 95. Many have wondered what
kinds of things that lost epistle contained. It might've been pretty similar to Colossians, the way Ephesians is similar to Colossians. It
might've concerned the same doctrines, but with different emphases
and specifics. It's fun to think about.

Which is good, since that's all we can do. That letter vanished
without a trace. When the time came to canonize the Bible, God made
sure that this letter didn't make it in. God made sure that this church—
spewed out of His mouth because they were lukewarm—would not
have their epistle preserved for the ages. Their place was wiped out,
and their city was destroyed and buried.

Chilling, isn't it? If God would do that to a whole town, what would He do to individual believers who make Him sick? Don't get all excited. I didn't say He revoked their salvation; I just said He wiped them out. I don't know about you, but I don't want an angry God coming after me when I've made Him sick to His stomach. Would you?

I believe that the Bible gives a hint as to why God might've let that epistle disappear. Check it out with me: "And say to Archippus, 'Take heed to the ministry which you have received in the Lord, that you may fulfill it'" (Colossians 4:17).

Another version of the verse reads: "Tell Archippus: 'See to it that you complete the work you have received in the Lord'" (NIV). Was Archippus part of the Laodicean fellowship? Was he the pastor there or chairman of the deacons? Did he complete the work that Paul mentioned? Did he heed the command he received from the Lord? Did the leaders at Laodicea fulfill their mandate from the hand of Christ?

I doubt it! Not when a mere thirty-five years later the Lord was ready to spit them into the dustbin of history.

THE LETTER WRITER

This letter to the Laodiceans in Revelation 3 came from the Son of God by the hand of the apostle John. So John, one of the original twelve, delivered that letter by APS (Apostolic Parcel Service). Now, that's plenty of authority from where I sit. If I received a letter like that, I can promise you I wouldn't let it sit in my "in" basket under a stack of junk mail. But just in case the folks at Laodicea didn't seem inclined to respect that level of authority, the One who wrote that letter described himself in three unique ways. Better listen up, church! "These things says the Amen, the Faithful and True Witness, the Beginning of the creation of God" (Revelation 3:14b).

We're talking about three aspects of Jesus Christ here that are absolutely fantastic.

He's the Amen

Do you realize that this is the only time in the whole Bible that Jesus Christ is specifically referred to as "the Amen"? This is an acknowledgement of that which is certain and valid. It is a word of human response to divine truth or divine action.

In the traditional black church, folks are all over this amen thing. You'll hear the pastor say, "Can I get an amen?" And the congregation jumps right in and says, "Amen, Pastor!" He doesn't have to beg for it, nobody's sleepin' at the switch or drawing pictures on the church bulletin. It's right there. And the more amens the pastor gets, the more encouraged he becomes in his preaching—until he's like a locomotive rollin' down the tracks under a full head of steam. He'll say, "Jesus is the answer to all your problems!" And the good folks in the congregation will shout back "Amen! Preach it!"

What are those people getting excited about when they say *amen*?

They're agreeing with the truth. They're lining up behind the pastor and saying, "Yes, we believe that what you say is right out of the Book. And not only do we believe it's the truth; we're going to line our lives up with that and start living the truth." That's what you're confessing when you say "amen" to the pastor's message.

Now, you'd better *not* say amen if it isn't biblical truth. Don't say amen just because it makes the pastor feel good. You don't want to find yourself lining up behind a lie. But if the words are true and based on the Book, then let your voice be heard! If not, button up.

Jesus *is* the Amen. Everything that comes from His lips is right and true, so you cannot disagree with what He says. If you do, you're rebelling against heaven, and you won't get very far! So when you line up behind everything Jesus says, when you say to Jesus, "Yes, Lord, yes! I'm changing my life to line up behind Yours," then you are acknowledging Him as the Amen. In turn, your whole life becomes an amen to the truth of Jesus Christ.

Isn't that exciting? Aren't you glad you're reading this book? Keep reading, because it just gets better!

Paul may be referring to Jesus as the "amen" in 2 Corinthians 1:20:

> For no matter how many promises God has made, they are "Yes" in Christ. And so through him the "Amen" is spoken by us to the glory of God. (NIV)

All the promises of God are *yes* in Him. How many? A-L-L.

What does that mean in the Greek? A-L-L.

This verse says that anything God has said will be done. It's right. It's true. He said it, He wills it, He wants it, and it's gonna happen. There's no discussion, no recount, no second opinion, and no court of appeal. Jesus isn't just the One who brings God's message; He *is* the Message, the Word, the fulfillment of all things. And when the way we live our lives says "amen" to *the* Amen, God gets the glory.

Amen?

This goes down hard in an era of moral relativism. A society that has rejected absolute truth just can't swallow it. It sticks in their craw, drives them nuts, and rubs their fur the wrong way. How can Jesus claim all truth? What makes His truth better than my truth or Buddha's truth?

It's very simple. He *is* truth. He told His disciples, "I am *the* way, *the* truth, and *the* life." No, that isn't politically correct, but guess what? If you can't accept this foundation stone of truth, Jesus becomes to you "a stone of stumbling and a rock of offense" (1 Peter 2:8). You're going to stumble, just as the church at Laodicea stumbled. Better get lined up behind the Amen. You don't want to be like Laodicea, because they never ever regained their feet.

He is the Faithful and True Witness

Okay, Laodiceans. Is that enough to shake you up a little? The Amen has spoken!

What's that? You need *more* proof? Well, He isn't only the Amen; He's also "the Faithful and True Witness." Here's a church that had so little truth and so little faithfulness hearing from Him who is 100 percent truthful and faithful.

When Jesus walked this earth, He gave witness to what He had seen and heard in His Father's house. The apostle John wrote: "No one has seen God at any time. The only begotten Son, who is in the bosom of the Father, He has declared Him" (John 1:18). Jesus has told us everything we need to know about the Father. As John the Baptist testified:

"He who comes from above is above all.... What He has seen and heard, of that He bears witness; and no one receives His witness. He who has received His witness has set his seal to this, that God is true. For He whom God has sent speaks the words of God; for He gives the Spirit without measure. The Father loves the Son, and has given all things into His hand." (John 3:31a, 32–35, NASB)

The One who is saying "I am not pleased with Laodicea" has been given everything by God the Father. You'd better know Him, and you'd better make Him a friend. What did David say in Psalm 2?

Serve the LORD with fear,
And rejoice with trembling.
Kiss the Son, lest He be angry,
And you perish in the way.
(Psalm 2:11–12)

Sounds like a great idea to me! Line up behind the Amen. That's the safest place in the whole universe. Line up behind the Faithful and True Witness. He makes a much better friend than an enemy.

If you had been in high school with me and had the opportunity to make me a friend, I guarantee you would have taken advantage of that. This was back in my B.C. (Before Christ) days, and if you weren't my friend, you just weren't very safe! If you bumped me in the hallway or even looked crossways at me, I could hurt you quick, do it any way I could, and feel warm and happy about it for the rest of the day.

Remember, the reason I went out for football was so that I could hurt white people legally. I was really a better baseball player than I was a football player. I had a tryout with the St. Louis Cardinals baseball team when I was fourteen years old. But it's more of a challenge to hurt people in baseball. You bean somebody with the ball, and *everybody* gets mad. In football, you can have at it on almost every play—which I did.

So if you had the opportunity to be Hutch's friend in high school, was it a smart thing to do? Oh yes. Line up behind me.

How much better to line up behind the Faithful and True Witness. How much better to walk in the shadow of our Elder Brother, the Son of God. Stand in His truth, walk in His truth, line up behind His truth, and no one in this world or the next can touch your soul.

If I were in the church of the Laodiceans, I'd be shakin' in my sandals by now. I'd be listening with my hands cupped around my ears so I wouldn't miss a word.

But Jesus wasn't yet finished reminding them of who He was.

He is the Beginning

He told the Laodiceans, "I am the Beginning of the creation of God."

He's the Beginning, He's the end, and He's all points in between. That's what He told John when He first appeared to him on the isle of Patmos: "I am the Alpha and the Omega, the Beginning and the End...who is and who was and who is to come, the Almighty" (Revelation 1:8).

Did you get that, John? Did you read that, churches? I am the *A* and I am the *Z*, and I am every letter in between. I'm the whole alphabet. Now, if I am the beginning and the end, then I have established for you through My Word what you've got to do from the beginning to the end of your Christian walk. I've got it all planned, first to last. You can relax and trust My plans for your life.

Isn't that smokin'?

He's the "author and finisher of our faith" (Hebrews 12:2). He's there in the beginning to launch you into the Christian life, He's there at the end to welcome you into His Father's house, and He's there all along the way to help you live for Him.

For the Laodiceans, He was there when the church was first established. He was there at their first meeting when they all joined hands and sang for joy over their salvation. He was at the beginning. And now it is very near the end, and He's there, too.

He says to the Laodiceans (and to all of us), "I have established what you need to do between the beginning of your life and the end of your life, in any aspect of every decision you make. You do not have the option to move outside what the Alpha and Omega, the great Amen, and the Faithful and True witness has said is the right thing to do."

He's the Almighty! I don't know about you, but it's enough for me to say that if the Almighty is going to dictate what's good and bad at all times, it ought to be my responsibility to line up with Him regardless of my circumstances.

Who is saying all these things to Laodicea—and to you and me? It is the One who was with God, the One who is God. He's the One who was from the beginning. He was before *before* and He'll be after *after*. And when *He* says the church should jump, the church needs to answer, "How high?"

HOT OR COLD?

"I know your works, that you are neither cold nor hot. I could wish you were cold or hot." (Revelation 3:15)

As for me and my house, I plan on being hot. Throw some water on me and see if I smoke!

I was hot when I first found the Lord, and I want to be even hotter as the days go by. This is no time to cool off. If Christ has set you on fire, stoke those flames. Keep burning. Stay hot. If you're lukewarm, if your fire has died down, watch out! You'd better find some lighter fluid *fast*.

There was a lot going on behind the scenes in these letters to the seven churches. We hear that phrase about "lukewarm" and think about lukewarm soup or lukewarm coffee. Don't you love it when you take a big swig of coffee and find it less than hot? (On the east side of Seattle, in the posh suburbs, they call that *tepid*.) You might feel like spitting it out, but if you're in public you probably swallow it and say, "Yuck, that stuff's terrible!" But the Laodiceans heard an even stronger message in the Lord's words.

The area around the city was known for its mineral springs. People would drink this water for medicinal purposes, but there was a catch: If they drank it hot, it would do them some good. If they drank it totally cold, it could still do them some good. But if they drank it lukewarm, it made them throw up! It would turn them inside out to drink that tepid, Laodicean water—everyone in town knew that.

For all its wealth, the city had to make do with a bad water system. A six-mile-long aqueduct brought Laodicea its supply of water from the south. If the water was piped from the mineral hot springs, it cooled to lukewarm before it reached the city. If it came from a cooler source, it got warmed up in the aqueduct on the way. Lukewarm again! Ten miles away in Colosse, the water was cool and refreshing.

Over in Hierapolis, the water was hot and good for medicine.

Laodicea, between Hierapolis and Colosse, was neither cold nor hot.

God says, "I can deal with those two types of people. I can deal with the heathen that don't know Me, and I can deal with folks that are on fire for Me and My kingdom." One group needs salvation, and the other needs encouragement. But what do you do with the lukewarm? What do you do with folks who claim to belong to Christ but think only of serving themselves?

As I mentioned in an earlier chapter, I am well aware that some singles in the Seattle area come to my church for one reason only: to meet other singles and form relationships. There are guys that show up wanting to prey on those sweet Christian women. And there are women who show up from time to time because they've heard there are some decent, eligible bachelors in this place.

These folks better hope I don't find out who they are, because I'll be on their case like cold on ice, dots on dice, and drugs on *Miami Vice!* The church of Jesus Christ is not a singles' club. Lukewarm believers with false motives make Him sick. I'll let you in on a little secret: What makes God sick makes me sick, too.

Christ was telling the Laodiceans, "Listen, people, you taste like that warm mineral water to Me. I put you there in that place—up in that beautiful city on a hill, right there along the main highway—to do some good. If you had brought My word and My salvation to your city, it would have been healing for the nations. It would have been medicine for the soul. But you aren't hot, and you aren't cold. You're something in between, and you aren't helping anyone. When I taste you—your halfhearted commitment, lukewarm love, partial purity, and tepid faithfulness—it makes Me want to throw up."

As a believer in Christ, your life is supposed to be different—distinct from the culture all around you. Your decisions should be different. Your attitudes should be different. Your speech should be different. Your lifestyle should be different. Your response to trials and difficult circumstances should be different. The way you handle money should be different. The way you relate to the opposite sex should be different. The very expression on your face should be different.

Do you still treat people the way you did as an unbeliever? Do you still try to get ahead of the next guy and climb the ladder and take advantage like you did as a nonbeliever? Do you still gossip and slander people? Do you still play around with sexual impurity?

Watch out! You're not putting a good taste in God's mouth. In fact, whenever a believer in Christ lives like the world, it makes God sick to His stomach. It grieves His Holy Spirit. And if a believer continues to live that way, God will bring stern correction into that life.

No normal parent wakes up in the morning with a desire to punish his child. He hopes to get through the day without having reason to use discipline to get his son or daughter back on the right track. Same thing with God—He does not delight in bringing punishment upon His own. In the book of Hosea, Scripture shows how God's emotions churned over the judgment He was about to bring to His rebellious people.

"How can I give you up, Ephraim?
How can I hand you over, Israel?...

My heart churns within Me;
My sympathy is stirred."
(Hosea 11:8)

His heart churns. His stomach turns. He doesn't like to do it...but "whom the LORD loves He chastens, and scourges every son whom He receives" (Hebrews 12:6). What's the bottom line for compromising, half-hearted believers? "I am the one who corrects and disciplines everyone I love. Be diligent and turn from your indifference" (Revelation 3:19, NLT).

HIS VIEW, OUR VIEW

"Because you say, 'I am rich, have become wealthy, and have need of nothing'—and do not know that you are wretched, miserable, poor, blind, and naked—I counsel you to buy from Me gold refined in the fire, that you may be rich; and white garments, that you may be clothed, that the shame of your nakedness may not be revealed; and anoint your eyes with eye salve, that you may see." (Revelation 3:17–18)

You say, "I am rich."

After a powerful earthquake destroyed many of their buildings in A.D. 17, the wealthy city of Laodicea required no imperial government help to rebuild. By the time they'd finished passing the hat around, they had enough money to rebuild it better than before.

The church there had deep pockets, too. Unlike other places I could mention, Laodicea had no problem meeting their church's budget demands. They could have all their potlucks catered, Jack. They could take their youth group around in fancy chariots. They could serve communion in gold cups and on silver plates. They could put their choir in hot new outfits. They could pay their pastor as much as the mayor! (Now *there's* a concept.)

When Christians from other towns came to visit, they could say, "Don't worry about putting anything in the offering plate, brother. We've got more than we can spend. Give your offering to Colosse— they could use a few bucks. Send an offering to Ephesus—they may be a little low, over there on the coast. But we're just fine."

They thought they were fine, anyway. But they weren't. No, not at all.

They were flat broke and didn't even know it.

They may have invested a lot of money, but they hadn't put it in the right mutual funds. They had lots of nice-looking stock certificates, but in Revelation 3 their market crashed, and they had nothing. Jesus said, "You didn't buy from Me, and you invested in the wrong things. Buy gold from Me that's been fired, that's pure, that'll last forever."

The apostle Peter once reminded a group of suffering believers— many of whom had lost everything—that they had an inheritance that nothing in this world could touch. It was a fortune that no stock market crash could threaten, no thief could steal, no crooked bank teller could embezzle, and no hurricane could blow away. In fact, it was reserved in God's own security deposit box in heaven.

In this you greatly rejoice, though now for a little while, if need be, you have been grieved by various trials, that the genuineness

of your faith, being much more precious than gold that per-
ishes, though it is tested by fire, may be found to praise, honor,
and glory at the revelation of Jesus Christ.
(1 Peter 1:6–7)

"You are wretched."

Wretched, huh? We don't use that word much these days. It's clear to
me that the Lord never enrolled in a sales training seminar. He never
attended a sensitivity course. He never read *How to Win Friends and
Influence People*. He didn't even take Evangelism 101. But you know
what? He doesn't seem a bit worried about stepping on anyone's toes
in this passage.

If you are wretched, you are more than bad. Wretched is *very* bad.
It's bad on steroids. Most likely, you don't feel inclined to run out and
look for friends who are wretched. "Oh, you are such a wretched person. Would you be my friend?" It might be different if you were
wretched yourself, and that was the only kind of person that would
hang around you.

The Laodiceans thought they were refined, tasteful, upper-crust
kind of people. That's because they hadn't looked in the Lord's mirror
for a while. If they had looked, they wouldn't have been happy with
what they saw. They might've turned green in the face.

"You are miserable."

The Lord also said they were miserable. Another way to say that is *pitiful.* If you are a very proud person, the last thing you want people to
call you is "pitiful." What's pitiful? A starved kitten is pitiful. A stray

dog that's been out in the rain all night is pitiful. A guy with a cardboard sign begging for money in a mall parking lot is pitiful. Pitiful is the kind of football team you don't want to play for—your fans wear sacks over their heads.

Pitiful is not good. That's what the Laodiceans were, and they didn't even know it.

"You are poor."

Poor? The Laodiceans would have laughed at that one. Have you seen my checking account? Have you seen my Mercedes? Have you checked out my portfolio? Have you talked to my broker? Have you seen what's been happening with my 401k?

I've talked to people like that. And do you know what I've noticed? One major heart attack will make them forget about every bit of money they have. One diagnosis of terminal cancer will make all their investments irrelevant. They'd give it all away in a heartbeat for another chance at life.

Jesus, the Lord of life, says, "You might have won the lottery. You might have won Publishers Clearing House and have a check waiting for you from Ed McMahon. But you are poor without Me. Better check those investments."

"You are blind."

Jesus wasn't talking to visually impaired people here. He was talking about spiritual eyes—eyes that stubbornly refuse to see the truth right in front of them. In John 9, after Jesus had healed a man of his physical blindness, He said, "For judgment I have come into this world, that those who do not see may see, and that those who see may be made blind" (v. 39).

Some of the Pharisees that were hanging around felt insulted. "Are we blind, too?" they asked Jesus.

Jesus said to them, "If you were blind, you would have no sin; but now you say, 'We see.' Therefore your sin remains" (v. 41).

"You are guilty," He told them, "of what you refuse to see." That goes for you and me, as well. If you are a lukewarm Christian today, you are guilty of what you refuse to see. Blame anybody else that you like—blame your circumstances; blame your parents; blame your attention deficit disorder. It all boils down to flat Y-O-U. Look in the mirror and see the biggest problem you've got.

"You are naked."

That would be a terrible sight for some of us! When Adam and Eve realized they were naked, they hid in the bushes, hoping that God might overlook them when He took His daily stroll through the Garden.

"Adam? Where are you?"

"Oh, Adam!" Eve whispered. "Here He comes!"

"Shush, woman! Get down behind that bush. Maybe He'll walk right by us."

"Well, Adam, you know, He *is* God."

"Shhh! Pipe down! If it wasn't for you, I wouldn't be in this mess!"

But we all know that a bunch of leaves couldn't hide Adam and Eve from the eyes of the Lord. These are eyes that "run to and fro throughout the whole earth," and before which "there is no creature hidden from His sight, but all things are naked and open to the eyes of Him to whom we must give account" (2 Chronicles 16:9; Hebrews 4:13).

If you are lukewarm in your heart today, you are laid bare before the Messenger to the church of Laodicea. You're deceived if you think otherwise. Regardless of how good you feel about what people tell you, you are buck naked before God.

Wretched…poor…miserable…blind…naked. That's the bad news. The good news is that if we realize our condition and come to Him in humility and repentance, He won't leave us like that!

THE REMEDIES OF JESUS

"I counsel you to buy from Me gold refined in the fire, that you may be rich; and white garments, that you may be clothed, that the shame of your nakedness may not be revealed; and anoint your eyes with eye salve, that you may see." (Revelation 3:18)

When you come to the feet of Jesus, when you line up behind the Amen, when you accept the testimony of the Faithful and True Witness, He never leaves you the way you were!

Are you wretched? That can be a good thing. *Wretched* also means to be "deeply afflicted, dejected, or distressed in body or mind." Have you been there? Are you there now? Stop pretending everything is okay. Stop living behind a plastic evangelical mask. Come to Jesus, and He will lift you up.

Are you spiritually bankrupt? Did you put all your money into Ukrainian savings bonds and find that your investments are now worthless? Invest in the Son of God. Invest in the Word of God and the people of God, and you'll build up capital that will still be gaining interest after the stars have fallen from the sky.

Are you blind? Is your spiritual vision foggy and distorted? Receive some first aid from the One who healed a blind man with a little dirt and a little spit. Laodicea was known across Asia Minor for its medical school—and for a medicinal salve that could cure certain diseases of the eyes.

Jesus told them, "You've been anointing your eyes with the wrong medicine. You've got the wrong prescription. You think you can see, but your vision is becoming worse and worse. You're looking at black and calling it white. You're looking at white and calling it black. Put on the salve of God. It soothes, it heals, and you'll see things as you've never seen them before."

Are you spiritually naked and ashamed before the Lord? Let Him clothe you in white, just as the father clothed his rebellious, prodigal son with the softest robe in the house. Laodicea was famous for its black sheep and for the clothing made from that black wool. Jesus said, "I've got a better color for you. Let Me clothe you in white, and I will take away all your shame."

I STAND AT THE DOOR

"Behold, I stand at the door and knock. If anyone hears My voice and opens the door, I will come in to him and dine with him, and he with Me." (Revelation 3:20)

You'd expect this last letter to the last church in the last book of the Bible to end with a fireball or an explosion of some kind.

Instead, it ends with a knock on the door.

With a gentle invitation.

The letter to the Laodiceans has been harsh—the harshest of the seven. God has taken these proud, wealthy believers and stripped them naked, revealing to themselves and the world exactly what they were. He told them that their lukewarm lifestyle—their casual, carnal, sleepy Christianity—made Him want to vomit. The church—and the city itself—was teetering on a cliff of utter destruction. Judgment! Judgment was about to fall. Laodicea would disappear from the face of the planet.

But what's that sound I hear?

Who's that knocking on the door?

It's Jesus Christ, still waiting to come in.

It's Jesus Christ, still waiting to save.

It's Jesus Christ, still ready to offer His friendship and fellowship and eternal protection.

There is no record that the church at Laodicea ever repented. But individuals from all over the world can still respond to Christ's knock on the door of their lives.

Remember how we began this book? We began with a picture of the Lord of the church bustin' through into our world to tell His household what it needs to do. And as we said, He has a perfect right to do that very thing. Why? Because He is the Bridegroom, the head of the bride. He needs no invitation because He belongs there. All authority has been given to Him by the Father. He who is the head of all believers has been delivering His warnings—and His promises—to the church in Revelation 2 and 3, and the church had better listen.

But now, at the close of His last letter to the last church, the Bible gives us a different picture. When it comes to restoring fellowship with His wandering, halfhearted, lukewarm children—the worst of the bunch, those about whom He could find no good thing to say—Jesus knocks at the door and waits. He doesn't kick in the door like a SWAT team commander. He doesn't hammer on it like a marshal with a subpoena or a collection agent after your last buck-fifty.

He knocks like a friend.

He taps on your door like someone who expects His knock to be recognized.

And He waits.

It doesn't matter where you've been, what you've done, or how you've done it. If you open the door, He will come in. If you welcome Him back to the center of your life, you will again experience His fellowship, just like in the old days.

The church members in Laodicea heard that knock, closed their ears, and turned away.

Laodicea missed its chance.

Don't miss yours.

A PROMISE
FOR OVERCOMERS

Until now, we haven't really talked about the rewards Jesus is offering to these churches. Now that we've reached the end of our time together, I think it would be appropriate to look at what's waiting for overcomers.

In every letter, Jesus promised a reward to those who heeded that which He had warned them about. To those who persevered in righteousness, He offered some of the greatest incentives in all the Bible. If God is pleased with you:

- You will eat from the tree of life, which is in the paradise of God;
- You will not be hurt by the second death;
- You will receive hidden manna to eat;
- You will be given a white stone with a new, secret name;
- You will be given rulership over the nations;
- You will be given the morning star;

- You will be clothed in white garments;
- Your name will remain in the Book of Life forever;
- Jesus Himself will confess your name before His Father and the angels;
- You will be a pillar in the heavenly temple of God, and you will never again have to leave His presence;
- Jesus will write on you the name of God, the name of the New Jerusalem, and His own new name; and
- You will sit together with Christ on His throne.

Not a bad benefits package, wouldn't you say?

THE BOTTOM LINE

I said earlier that if you want to know what someone thinks, you ought to just ask him. Well, that's what we've done in this book: We've asked Jesus what He thinks of the church today. God's so smokin'—He knew we'd ask that question, and He made sure the answer got written down so we could find out.

So what's the conclusion? After surveying all seven churches of Asia Minor and applying their lessons, what can we say Jesus thinks about us as we begin the third millennium of the church age?

The bottom line is this: The church is not doing well. Over 71 percent (that's five out of seven churches) are in need of rebuke. To me, that means that 71 percent of the people in churches need repentance. And it probably also means that 71 percent of me is in need of repentance, too.

Let's not worry about "those other people" right now. Let's just concentrate on you and me. I know I have my Sardis days—those days when I rest on reputation and past victories. I don't really feel like seeking God on those days. How about you?

I've had my share of Pergamum days, too. On Pergamum days I'm a hypocrite. I chastise people for the smallest of sins, then embrace utter depravity in my own life.

Sometimes I'm living in Ephesus. On Ephesus days I leave my first love in the dust and go over to things I think will please me more than Jesus Christ could. My flesh doesn't like living under anyone else's authority, not even His.

On my Thyatira days I tolerate error when I hear it in the church. I know it's wrong; I know I ought to do something about it. But I'm just too weary. Why do I always have to right the wrongs of the world? I'll get to it next time. Maybe somebody else will do what ought to be done.

Other days I'm lukewarm. Those Laodicea days may be the worst. I don't wallow in sin but neither can I motivate myself to cry out to God. Those are my blah days, my couch potato days. I'm in a fog of apathy, and if I could spit me out of my own mouth, I would.

Praise God that I have other kinds of days, too! Smyrna days, when I am counted worthy to suffer for His name; and Philadelphia days, when I walk through doors of opportunity wedged open by the great Locksmith. Even on my darkest days there are parts of me that have not defiled their garments, parts that do not buy into the doctrine of Balaam or the sin of Jezebel. In my heart of hearts, I cling to the Cross despite my sin.

And always there is Jesus, standing in love and holiness, offering hope: "I know your pain, my child. I know your good works. I've seen what those false brothers have done to you. I know your love and your patience and your faith. You are Mine and I have great rewards for you if you'll come on back in line with My will.

"But I love you too much to let you remain like this. I'm your King and your Savior, and I've seen where you've left the narrow path and wandered into lust and apathy and fear. Come back…wake up! Walk straight, so that when I come in judgment, you will be spared from My chastisement and will rule with Me on My throne and never again leave My presence."

It is my prayer that you have heard from our Lord in these pages and that as you reread Revelation 2 and 3 you will continue to find yourself in one or another of those ancient churches. We all want to live in Philadelphia and have their opportunities. But sometimes we have to live in the persecution of Smyrna or even where Satan's throne is. Even there, though, in this world that Satan rules, we can hear the voice of the Alpha and Omega breaking through to bring us comfort, discipline, and hope.

Multnomah Publishers

The publisher and author would love to hear your comments about this book. *Please contact us at:*
www.multnomah.net/beforeall

"Get filled up, fueled up, prayed up, fired up...
then go out into the world and give witness."

—Ken Hutcherson

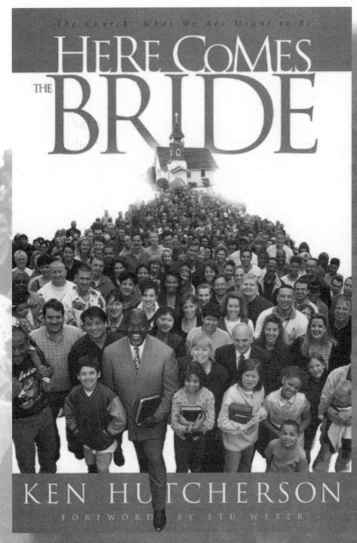

Ken Hutcherson reveals how God's original intention for His church has
been distorted by tradition, denominationalism, racism, and fear, and how
we can discover God's will for us when we strip away those elements.

ISBN 1-57673-359-9